STU

WHEELS OF THUNDER

INPIRED BY A TRUE ACCOUNT OF LIFE WITH A LIEARNING DIFFICULTY

Printed in the United States of America
ISBN: Softcover 978-1-63871-853-6
eBook 978-1-63871-854-3
Republished by: PageTurner Press and Media LLC
Publication Date: 01/06/2022

To order copies of this book, contact:
PageTurner Press and Media
Phone: 1-888-447-9651
info@pageturner.us
www.pageturner.us

WHEELS OF THUNDER

CONTENTS

Chapter One

The Beginning of a Legend

For all the racing drivers in the world, the greatest thrill was speed. For part-time amateur mechanic and wannabe racing driver Stuart Robson, this was something of a lifetime ambition. He had always dreamt of winning a race with a touring race car. Stuart himself was a twenty-one-year old with a love of speed and cars running so deep that people even said that his brain was shaped like a Formula One car. He had spent most of his life in love with vehicles of all shapes and sizes, but people couldn't understand his strange ways and superior knowledge of things way outside of his age group. When he was at primary school his teachers would often complain to his parents at how very behind he was in his schoolwork. His maths was very poor and English literature even more so.

Both his teachers and parents thought him dyslexic, so he was allowed extra time and assistance in order to complete all of his work. His schoolwork looked poor, and his parents worried that he was doomed for the rest of his life. But by the time he was seven years old (still not being able to complete a primary school SATs test) he could completely strip down and rebuild a motorcycle engine, even though most of his classmates had just about mastered basic number sums. At twelve years old he finished the whole motorcycle itself, and by the time he finished school at eighteen he had managed to complete two restoration projects for his family, including a classic 1969 military Series Two Land Rover and a 1956 Fordson Major Tractor.

For most of his younger childhood and for some years afterwards into secondary school, Stuart was avoided by his peers because they found him strange, surrounded in mystery, and most of the time just plain old-fashioned weird. Then on his eleventh birthday in the freezing cold month of January, when he had just finished another two-hour stint alone in the shed at the bottom of the garden, Stuart discovered the truth about himself that had been hidden from him for so long. His parents feared that if he had known the truth any earlier he would have attempted to take in his own life in shame, as was the case with so many people born with learning difficulties. The condition he had been born with was the very rare learning difficulty called Asperger's Syndrome, which was on the autistic spectrum.

His parents had hidden it from him for so long that Stuart didn't know what to do with himself anymore after failing to satisfy everybody he knew that he could live independently for the rest of his life. After being told about his autism, Stuart devoted the next decade of his life to learning about his condition but found that there was no cure for it. The only thing he knew that he was good at was driving. For all of his life, his complete ambition had been to become a lorry driver with the famous haulage company Eddie Stobart.

And so it was that fifteen years later he found himself doing the same thing he'd seen countless racing drivers doing all those years ago. It was at that moment the now twenty-one-year-old Stuart Robson woke with a start, sweating all over at the terrible dream he'd just been having.

It took him a few seconds to realise what he had seen in his dream.

There had been a white BMW race car, which he didn't recognise. Weirdly, he was the one who had been driving it. He racked his brains again in an attempt to remember even just a small part of his vision, but it was no good. Sitting up slowly, he closed his eyes and placed what he could remember to the back of his mind into the area he called his 'mind box'. The mind box was a very clever piece of mental problem-solving equipment which he had used for some years. It was a way of storing information inside the many layers of his memory banks so that when he really needed it, the information was easily accessible. A safe haven for his thought and memories as most would say in their professional capacity as what humanity deemed 'normal'. If he then used his Asperger's as well, he could amplify his thinking power in order to visualise a particular scene or source of information to use at whatever time and place was necessary.

Stuart himself was just under six foot tall and well built, with average-length brown hair that always seemed to have a mind of its own. When he ran a comb through it his parents used to joke that he looked like Tom Cruise from the well-known 1980s film *Top Gun.* In terms of likeness and cool rating by most people's standards, he would be best described by the BBC's television programme *Top Gear* as 'Seriously Un-Cool'. He also had a great fear of crowds and social events, like weddings and nightclubs, because of the overwhelming fact that he didn't understand the world as everyone else did.

To his family and friends he was just plain ole run-of-the-mill Stuart, but the outside world never fully accepted him. From a young age, his classmates would often steer clear of him, believing rumours that people with his condition were dangerous individuals who would go on the attack at the slightest sound or touch. In support of this idea, on his sixteenth birthday his best friend, Ben, had given him a friendly tap on the shoulder from behind only to find himself on the floor a second later because Stuart had jumped so much he had knocked his poor, confused friend backwards into the dining room table. Stuart quickly apologised, realising his best friend wasn't likely to attack him from behind – especially not on his birthday.

It was all complete nonsense, of course, along with the superstition about the state of such individuals with his condition. Successfully locking the dreamed crash scene in the back of his mind, Stuart pushed back the bed covers. As he did so he gazed over at the corner of the room, and what he saw made him jump about a foot in the air and make to pull the duvet cover back over himself as quickly as possible, as he never wore any pyjamas whilst in bed. Standing in the corner of the room, quite out of place from the model cars, various pictures, and posters on the walls, was a beautiful brown-haired woman. At first Stuart was unsure of what to do. Maybe it was just a long-forgotten memory that had been stored away in the back of his mind. He seemed to be mesmerised by her for a second, not in a sexual way but in confusion.

It was weird to have this thought. Something nagging in his head was telling him that he had seen her before. Where had he seen her before, and why was she here now, in his slightly dark bedroom? He would put her age in around her early twenties, exactly the same age as Stuart. She smiled at that moment, showing bright white teeth whilst throwing back her head so her shoulder-length hair flew in all directions before falling down again. It almost looked like she couldn't see him. But then again, she must have been able to see him because she was staring right at him. Stuart grinned to himself and looked away for a second just to hide his face from her.

You know, if this is a memory, I like it, and I never knew I had it, thought Stuart, agreeing with himself. He looked back up again and was shocked to see only the dark corner of his bedroom. The strange woman with her shoulder-length brown hair must have been a vision, because she had vanished almost into thin air. He was taken aback at the sudden disappearance of the figure but shook himself all the same. He had to go to work in a few hours, so he pushed back the bedclothes and started to pull on a T-shirt and a pair of grubby jeans for work before walking out of the bedroom door down the stairs towards the faint smell of breakfast now wafting in through his bedroom door. The memory of the woman with brown hair, or 'the angel', as Stuart came to know it, stuck around in his mind for a few days as his normal, average life carried on around him.

Chapter Two

UB40 and the Death of Beatty Bathrooms Ltd

Every day Stuart would come downstairs to breakfast with the usual news on the television of a war going on somewhere in the Middle East or someone who had been brutally murdered down some narrow London street. His work life wasn't any better. It was thanks to Stuart and his specialist knowledge of mechanics and driving that all of the machinery in the warehouse where he worked in his hometown in Hertfordshire was still in fine working order. His fellow colleagues were at a complete loss as to how Stuart wasn't able to even complete a simple task like making a cup of tea and yet would manage to pull off a complete strip-down and rebuilding of anything mechanical, like a forklift truck—which was more complex than tea making ever was.

His governor had cleverly referred to this mystery as 'the Sherlock Holmes theory' because he knew very little about Stuart. At first his work colleagues found him a bit odd because of his unusually high knowledge of some things and hardly any knowledge of the others, but they had to admit after a while it did come in handy having someone like Stuart around. From Stuart's view, today was just a normal working day. It was a Friday, or in his opinion the best day of the week, because it was the start of the weekend the very next day. He'd found himself in a good corner that morning. As usual in his place of work, the forklift had gone wrong again. A few hours ago it had just stopped because of a fault somewhere in its depths.

A quick diagnostic on Stuart's part had reported that the emergency brake connection had snapped and all the brakes had jammed on and wouldn't budge. It was the perfect excuse to not have to talk to anyone for a couple of hours whilst he got it fixed, so it suited him down to the ground. Nothing, however, could have prepared him for what happened next.

'Hey, Stu. How's the fork truck looking?' said a voice right behind him. Stuart jumped so much he hit his head on the underside of the raised canopy. He pulled himself out from underneath, blinking like mad because small lights had started popping in front of his eyes. He tried to refrain from swearing at the person who had just made him jump and found his colleague Jack, known to the warehouse boys as JA, standing beside him with both arms folded, leaning up against some warehouse racking a few feet away.

'Damn it, Jack, don't do that, buddy,' said Stuart, rubbing the spot where he had hit his head on the underside of the forklift.

'Sorry, Stu. Daryl just wanted to know how Operation Extremely Time-Consuming Forklift Repair was going,' said Jack, standing up to walk over to the forklift and gaze down into the large area that Stuart had managed to clear in stripping out major parts. Parts of all shapes and sizes lay all over the floor as Stuart tried to get at the emergency brake settings.

'Well, I think it's about time that our managing director realised that we can only go as fast as he gives us the time and the equipment that we need in order to do the job,' said Stuart, a little put out at the fact that the boss of the company wanted a complex and time-consuming job done quickly.

Does he think that mechanics is simple? thought Stuart to himself. He quickly took on a calm voice when he next spoke to Jack. Stuart always made an effort to keep him onside, as he was thoughtful and understanding. Being bought up at the same time as Stuart, Jack was a hands-on person, very practical, and not afraid of standing up to anyone who insulted him or anyone else.

'As for his question of how long it's going to take, I'm having a guess at least a good twenty-four hours, if not longer.' Stuart pointed down into the hole where a single cable lay loose amongst all of the others. It was this small metal cable that was supposed to jam the brakes on if the emergency electrics cut in, bringing the forklift to a complete stop.

So far all that had happened was the emergency would cut in, and instead of stopping dead it would keep rolling. 'Well, we both know that our friend Captain Chaos the Boss has somewhat of a severe attitude problem towards most people,' said Stuart quietly, hoping not to be overheard by anyone except for Jack standing beside him.

Jack gave a short laugh before retracting his head from out under the forklift and coming face to face with none other than the boss himself, who was only a few feet away staring at amazement at the amount of parts and tools that were spread in Stuart's work space. Being autistic, Stuart had laid a lot of the tools and parts down in a particular place and labelled them so not to forget where each part went and at what time it would be needed.

'I would like a word with you both when Stuart's quite finished destroying my forklift, said Daryl, having only just walked into the conversation. Stuart, who had half expected Daryl to walk round the corner at any moment, didn't jump or exclaim loudly but pulled himself out from underneath the forklift and glared at Daryl so darkly that it was as if he had committed a dreadful and unforgiveable crime. Stuart and Daryl had got on quite well to start off with when he first joined the company. Eighteen months on, however, Stuart and Daryl's relationship had deteriorated badly. A month earlier Daryl had accused Stuart in a very aggressive way of dangerous driving with the forklift truck when he had no proof of this stupid accusation whatsoever.

Since this incident the company had gone sharply downhill, resulting in several other members of staff resigning their posts as well as seriously aggravating the other members of staff who still worked for him. As it turned out, there was a secret bet on that the first person who told Daryl that he was an idiot to his face would receive thanks from every member of staff for extreme bravery. Back in the warehouse Stuart wiped his hands on a bit of old rag he had before following Jack up the stairs in Daryl's overlarge office.

'What's the betting he's got some stupid idea that we all have to follow? Remember that one where he put in a door and wall downstairs then locked the door and put a sign saying nobody could use it?' said Stuart as Jack let out a small laugh and opened the door to Daryl's office.

Daryl sat behind his desk looking tired. He tried to look his best to be happy even though Jack was twiddling his thumbs in his lap and Stuart was still looking at Daryl with something remarkably like pure hatred. 'I think you both know the situation with the company at this current moment in time; our work has seriously dropped off, and we are starting to lose serious money,' said Daryl, trying to keep his voice straight and level. Stuart could see that Daryl's left hand was shaking on the desk. Jack was still twiddling his thumbs in his lap but was taken aback when Daryl asked him to step outside for a moment. Jack stood up and told Daryl he would make a cup of tea for them before lightly tapping Stuart on the shoulder and leaving through the door.

Daryl thanked Jack as he left before turning to Stuart, who was still sitting in one of the chairs. His frown had slightly disappeared, but he was shocked when Daryl sighed and rubbed his eyes with his hands almost as if he were bracing himself for a sudden piece of bad news. 'First of all, Stuart, I want to thank you for all your hard work. If you hadn't been around I'd be snowed under with maintenance bills by now. I don't think I've ever seen anyone able to do more mechanical repairs than you have.'

Stuart was still silent, but he noticed something in Daryl's voice that he hadn't heard before. 'The company's folding, isn't it?' said Stuart, trying to keep his voice calm. He had come quite close to announcing on a number of occasions in recent weeks that he saw Daryl as someone who thought he was a good manager but in all honesty couldn't have organized a snail for a slow race.

Daryl sat up straight so quickly he almost sent the desk flying. 'How do you know about that?' demanded Daryl, looking angry and wondering who had told Stuart about this piece of confidential information.

'You shouldn't leave important documents like that lying around where anyone can see them,' answered Stuart. As usual, he was focussing on the details that other people would have overlooked. Daryl looked down at his desk. Paperwork littered it from end to end, but on the opposite end were some official-looking letters from a number of companies claiming that Daryl's company owed them a considerable amount of money and threatening court action if he didn't pay up.

'Well spotted, Stuart,' said Daryl, scooping up the letters and shoving them in a drawer before facing Stuart again. 'We're shutting up shop at the end of next week. I've done everything I can, but it seems the company is going too far downhill to stop it,' said Daryl. At that moment Stuart, for only for a fleeting second, felt sorry for him. But after what had happened in the past, there was too much disrespect to overcome for the man who now sat before him.

Jack opened the door at the very moment carrying three cups of tea. He put one down in front of Daryl, handed another to Stuart, and took a sip from the third. Stuart and Daryl thanked Jack for the tea.

'Jack, sorry to send you off again, but is it okay if I have a minute with Stuart?' asked Daryl suddenly out of the blue.

'Sure,' said Jack, sounding okay. But once his back was to them he seemed edgy. He strode across the office and exited through the door as Daryl turned back to Stuart.

For a second they both stood there in silence. Stuart glared at him like a destroyer of worlds. Daryl looked worried, trying to think what to say next.

'I know this hasn't been easy for any of us, but I know what you're going through,' said Daryl. But he instantly stopped dead at Stuart's anger.

'How I feel? You won't have the first idea how I feel right now,' said Stuart, who was struggling to refrain from shouting at what felt like his archenemy.

'I do have a son with the same condition. I know what I'm doing,' said Daryl in response but then realised too late that he had said the wrong thing. There was an almighty bang as Stuart's clenched fist made contact with the wooden desk so hard that all of the pens in the stationary pot tipped over and rolled away over the already overcrowded desk.

'How dare you? I've never been so insulted in my life. You wouldn't know the first damn thing about autism if it stripped itself down to its underwear and danced in front of you,' shouted Stuart so loudly that even the voices coming from the upper floor where the office staff were went quiet. It seemed they didn't need to sneak around downstairs to hear what was being said.

Daryl didn't reply, but his mouth had dropped open in shock. Stuart never shouted or said insulting things to anyone, and yet here he was telling Daryl he was practically a Class One idiot. 'You know what? I should have done this a long time ago,' said Stuart as he stuck his finger up at him in a typical 'up yours' style before strolling across the room and throwing open the door, allowing it to bang shut behind him.

'He's laying us both off,' exclaimed Jack ten minutes later back in the warehouse office with Stuart. Both were drinking their cups of tea. Jack had taken the news worse than Stuart, as he was living in a rented flat. If money wasn't coming in for him, he would be out on the streets.

'Daryl's trying to make out that the company hasn't made a great success of itself when the real truth is a simple case of poor management and trying to take on more than we can deal with,' replied Stuart, taking another swig of tea.

'Well, I guess that puts us both on the UB40 list,' said Jack, grinning from ear to ear as he finally had a chance to put Daryl and the company behind him for good.

'I concur ol-boy,' answered Stuart in a mock posh voice, which he was as good at these days, as he downed his cup of tea and smacked his lips.

'That, Jack, was the best cup of tea I have had in a long time, and I thank you many times for it,' said Stuart, placing his mug back down onto the table. Unemployment soon came to Jack, Stuart, and the others from Beatty's Bathroom Limited, as they all received redundancies a week later.

Giving the old, grubby-looking warehouse one last grateful look, Stuart smiled and turned away, driving away into the sunset and into the future. With Beatty's Bathroom Limited now flushed down the pan for good, it felt like months of hell had finally passed, and a brighter and more brilliant future was shining through for him. To his and everyone else's utter amazement, Daryl approached Stuart on the last day and asked him to come back and work for him when he set up again.

At this point Stuart told him to do something which he would never have said in front of his family and friends and promptly finished off his angry controlled outburst with the words 'Go to hell. You're evil.' This, it seemed, settled the matter once and for all. When it all boiled down to rock bottom, Daryl had ruined Stuart, not the other way round. But even after all of the bad management, Daryl still seemed to think that he'd done the right thing and that other people had just been sore losers about it. It was a miracle that everybody hadn't revolted against him and forced him to step down. As Stuart had always said to other people, 'Revolutions have solved many a problem in the past.'

Chapter Three

A Sprinter Called 'Road Runner'

Stuart had only just realised that this was to be the start of something exceptional. The months to come were to be the best of his life. With Daryl and the horror of his previous job now behind him and with a better future in store, Stuart started job hunting.

Six months had passed since Daryl and Stuart had met in his office back in the grubby warehouse in his hometown in Hertfordshire. After leaving Beatty's Bathroom Limited, Stuart had started working for a local Hertfordshire company called Perfect Bathrooms Ltd. It was just what Stuart had wanted for a long time. After being in the working world for over three years, he was finally where he wanted to be: in a driving job, and not just any driving job.

Perfect Bathrooms Limited on its front cover was selling high-end bathroom items to showrooms and warehouses all over the world. But the real genius of it all came from the head office in Hertfordshire. In Stuart's mind, life couldn't have been more perfect. He was in a driving job which was not only renowned for its almost military quality but because of its workplace attitude. He had been the first person taken on there in over five years because nobody was leaving. As a driver Stuart had been assigned to one of Perfect Bathrooms' most elite units. Nicknamed the 'Iron Eagles', they were highly trained, easy-going, and always made a perfect team when it came to working together. But the team itself was only half the story.

Having been given the call sign 'Captain Maverick', Stuart had been assigned the difficult tasks of long-distance and specialised load transportation. This required planning, skill, and careful driving, which he had in bucket loads thanks to his incurable autism. But his love wasn't the job that paid a salary or his ever-understanding colleagues. It was, in his opinion, the best van ever built, which had been his since the very beginning. It had been given the name 'Road Runner' because of its newfound speed and also because of the number plates in the window that read the same thing. It was a German-built Mercedes-Benz Sprinter 313 CDI that had started life with a 2.1-litre diesel engine but recently been upgraded to a 2.5-litre turbo diesel for extra power.

On this particular day, or 'mission', as most tended to like to refer to things, Stuart found himself heading home after a long drive to Bristol in the early hours of the morning. On these sort of trips, which mainly involved sitting on the motorways for long periods of time, Stuart found himself doing his favourite pastime: watching the many juggernaut articulated lorries that filled Britain's roads these days. He watched their many wheels turning over as he passed slowly by, occasionally getting a funny look from a speeding car or two. Still, he had to admit, after twenty miles a motorway could become a little dull at times.

The legendary Road Runner wagon, teamed with an endless amount of country-and-western music and Stuart's very own aviator sunglasses, made for an unusual sight. Among the many pieces of kit on the van, such as cruise control and satellite navigation (known to him as 'Sally'), was a state-of-the-art radio, which could be operated by a handheld connector. Sitting with his speed just above 65 mph on the speedometer, Stuart disconnected the handheld from the dashboard and pushed the button on the side.

'Trip check. Time authenticate 7.13am, ETA to home base fifty-eight minutes,' said Stuart, hanging the handle back on the dashboard.

'Acknowledged your position, Road Runner. Please be advised that you have heavy traffic on approach to home base in areas between eighteen and twenty-five. Over.' The voice that replied was that of the transport desk, which tracked all vehicle whereabouts and conditions as well as maintaining effective communication with its drivers. Passing underneath the motorway gantry, Stuart read the signs carefully. His next turning point was into the filter lane on the left, which took him from the M4 to the M25 towards Watford, the M1, and other major routes to the north of London. Sure enough, the traffic started to build up around Watford. But it wasn't as bad as expected, so Stuart made his ETA of fifty-eight minutes. He rolled up in the yard to the sound of working machines, such as the two forklifts, running at breakneck speeds all over the place, trying to keep up with the day's work. Pulling up in the yard, Stuart jumped down from the cab, still wearing his aviator sunglasses, and was instantly greeted by the yard operator.

This was a man by the name of Gary Grahams who instinctively and in a jokey sort of way raised his hand to his forehead in an American-style salute. Stuart kindly returned it with another salute. 'Captain Maverick reporting as ordered, sir,' he said in his convincing posh pilot voice, which he always used for general humour and morale purposes. Having taken down a full vanload, of products Stuart had returned with three decent-sized pallets, which had been transferred by the other branch to head office for company and customer use.

'Open her up, Captain. We'll tip it once the lorry's out of the yard,' said Gary. Stuart took off his sunglasses and clipped them to his T-shirt so they hung down the middle. Throwing open his doors, he strolled inside the warehouse, shouting the usual greetings to all those who worked there.

He reached the office and pushed the door open to sort out all of his paperwork from the day's driving. A number of in and out trays littered the walls, saying things like 'out and in delivers' and 'recirculation jobs' alongside 'new orders' and 'previous days'. As usual, Stuart ran his finger along the shelf until he came across a tray marked 'transfer papers' before slotting the tickets inside as if posting a letter. He heard a sudden revving engine and a hiss of air as the lorry that was being unloaded in the yard moved slowly forward out of the gate onto the road, taking a wide turning swing out to avoid hitting the trailer against the gate. By the time he had reached his van back in the yard, he was amazed to see that it had been offloaded with incredible speed, even though he had only been a few minutes.

'Thanks, boys,' called Stuart across the yard to the forklift operators parked up on the other side of the yard. They waved back at him as he jumped back into the cab and started the engine. Turning the van around, he headed straight out of the open gate, now feeling a lot lighter than he had been before. Within ten minutes of leaving the yard he was swinging into the narrow country lane which came out on a small farmhouse where he lived with the rest of his family. His van would often knock off any branches from the overhanging trees up the country lane but never seemed to scratch the white paintwork. Road Runner splashed in a puddle as Stuart made his way up the lane and swung into the farmyard in his usual parking space. The engine thudded into silence as Stuart turned the key into the off position and pulled it out of the ignition.

He jumped down from the cab, closing the door behind him and pressing a small button on his key. Two beeps came from Road Runner, and the indicators flashed as the van locked itself. Stuart made for the front door of the farmhouse. Letting himself in, he hung the van keys up on a hook by the door, which also housed all the keys of the other vehicles on the small farm. The usual thing to do would have been to have a shower and then go to bed until lunchtime, when his mother would come back from the school where she worked as a teaching assistant. But Stuart didn't feel tired, though he had been up since half past two that morning. He often found that he didn't get as tired as other people. It was quite amusing sometimes, watching his family falling asleep in front of the television every night whilst he stayed wide awake.

Making up his mind, Stuart turned on the spot, almost like a soldier on parade, and reopened the front door. He scooped up the keys to his favourite grey corrugated titanium barn on the opposite side of the road from the farmhouse. Making sure that his brother wasn't coming up the lane at breakneck speed with his car, he crossed the road and inserted a key into the heavy-duty padlock which held the two huge doors shut. Unlocking the padlock, he let it swing on the handle whilst he slid the doors open, allowing light to flood into the dark barn. Spread throughout the barn sat all the farm's machinery and equipment, which was repaired and maintained by Stuart.

These included the classic military Land Rover, the Fordson Major tractor, and Stuart's Harley Davidson motorcycle, which was covered under a huge sheet to stop it from getting dusty. A gleam of chrome could be seen from under the sheet. Stuart smiled to himself at the sight. He was rather fond of his Harley motorcycle and wouldn't let anyone touch it unless they had very clean hands and no dirt on their clothes. As it turned out, the inside of the barn was so clean that the floor seemed to shine back at him, revealing a gleaming surface. There was not an oil spill or spec of dirt anywhere on it. But the object that was of most interest to Stuart today wasn't the classic farm vehicles or his own beloved motorcycle but what looked like the sub frame of a high-performance car propped up on several lumps of wood made out of old railway sleepers.

The many parts of the stripped-out car were stacked on shelves all around the walls. The driver's and passenger doors and the boot cover were a dark blue colour soon to painted over. Being autistic since birth, Stuart had labelled all of the parts on the shelves according to where they went on the car and in what order. He always had a plan.

Stuart walked forward and ran his hand along the sub frame, which had been sandblasted back to its original grey factory colour, ready for re-spraying. A large tin of crystal white paint sat on the floor ready to be poured into the paint gun, which was hanging from the frame. On the bench on the far right of the barn was an old-fashioned Windows 98 computer. A file open on its screen was marked 'Thunderbolt'.

Clicking on the screen, Stuart opened the folder and found the file he was looking for. It showed a picture of a BMW M3 hardtop coupe built between 2000 and 2006, which was painted in an ocean blue colour with silver-coloured alloy wheels. The computer-edited picture showed a complete strip-down and rebuild of the whole car itself. It had several heavy modifications including a new, larger, and more powerful engine along with a big wing racing spoiler finished off with several sponsorship decoys, which included the family's business name, 'Robson Transport'. Moving away from the computer, Stuart admired the rest of the barn, which included the many cabinets and cupboards full of his tools. These were stacked neatly in every drawer according to their size, weight, and purpose.

Smiling to himself, Stuart closed the barn doors and walked back to a workbench fastened to the wall. He sat himself down on the chair by the workbench and began to reassemble some of the parts under a small lamp, which was attached on a spring-loaded holder to the wall by the side of the open Haynes complete strip-down and rebuild manual. Having Asperger's Syndrome, Stuart tended to look at the pictures rather than reading the written instructions. Although in most people's eyes this would have been a big mistake, he was such a wiz with mechanical things that it didn't take long to figure it all out.

Even after several days the frame still remained just a chassis frame. All of the other parts had been reassembled elsewhere and brought altogether in the barn to be put back into place like a giant air fix kit.

Stuart kept the barn locked and bolted so that nobody would go in and see what he was building. Even when the barn wasn't locked, the half-finished, custom-made BMW was covered under a thick sheet and the paperwork hidden away so nobody saw what he was doing. As Stuart sat at his bench after day five of the rebuild, finishing off the brake calliper unit, there was a small knock on the barn door. Stuart spun round quickly, letting the cover fall over the BMW frame, as his mother, Abigail Robson, walked round the half-closed door.

Chapter Four

Thunderstruck

'Unauthorised access requesting permission to enter,' said Abigail's voice from the doorway. Stuart relaxed a little, as the sheet now covered the whole car, hiding it from view.

'Permission granted,' said Stuart, who was leaning against the sheeted car. Darkness had started to fall outside, and the faint smell of baking was wafting in through the open barn doors from outside.

'Dinner's ready, Stuart; I hope you're coming in now,' said Abigail, looking Stuart up and down like a bossy housekeeper searching for signs of dirt. Stuart himself was wearing his normal light-blue boiler suit. It was covered in dirt smears, as he had been underneath the BMW reconnecting all of the electrical systems, which were crucial to all of the on-board systems he had installed.

Abigail walked away, leaving Stuart to quickly slip out of his boiler suit and wipe his hands on a bit of old rag before making his way towards his dinner, which had already been sitting on the table for a number of minutes beforehand. The family always dined together at a large wooden table in the living room which had been put together by David Robson using huge Victorian wooden beams taken out of a pub in the West Country when they dismantled it almost a decade ago. The memory of those beams always came back to Stuart very vividly. He had only been eleven at the time. His dad, David Robson, had loaded the timber into the trailer hitched behind the Land Rover, not realising Stuart had accidentally unhitched the trailer from the Land Rover's tow ball.

The trailer had rolled backwards straight over David's foot. But it hadn't stopped there; after running over David's foot it had kept rolling away, with Stuart still holding onto the trailer's A-frame. The resulting injury had left him a bit shaken, but afterwards he thought it had been a lot of fun being towed away by a two-hundred-kilogram trailer. He had always been told that it was vehicles that pulled trailers and not trailers that pulled people.

As the flashback ended, Stuart seated himself at the table as tonight meal's was placed down. It was the family favourite, chicken pie and mash with selected vegetables. Over dinner, it was the usual family tradition to discuss a certain topic. They would all take it in turns to choose whatever was on the list to be debated.

Potential topics included everything from items on the news to funny articles in the newspaper. Tonight it was David's turn, and the topic of choice was his well-earning business, which he had started in the year that Stuart was born. He had spent most of the day flicking through magazines and surfing the Internet looking for a good deal on a new van he was purchasing. As this wasn't David's specialised area, his next comment went in Stuart's direction.

'I could have done with you today, Stuart. I need to get some new fleet vehicles, but I can't think of what to buy. The Sprinters are way too far outside of the budget, I don't like the feel of the new Traffic vans, and the Ivecos that we've currently got are rusting away like mad,' said David, sounding like a man running out of options.

'There's the new Ford Transit Customs; they're a little smaller than the other vans, but they come with all sort of gadgets and very low fuel consumption as well,' replied Stuart before taking a bite out of a slice of bread. As usual, he was thinking out loud.

David had thought about not having more gadgets in his vans. But under the pretence of helping the company forward into the twenty-first century, he considered it. 'I never thought of getting a Transit. I'll look into it. Thanks, Stu. We'll take a look at them this weekend,' said David, reaching over and patting his eldest son on the shoulder as a way of saying thank you.

The Transit Custom vans hadn't been out very long, so when David and Stuart went over to the nearest dealer they didn't have one there to view. However, David decided to take Stuart's advice. Sure enough, several days later three brand new Transit vans arrived at the Robson Transport headquarters in company livery, ready for commercial use. David Robson may have only been a small company man, but he had a reputation for getting the job done, even it took him longer than others. This trait had been passed onto his eldest son; Stuart was just as determined as his father and his grandfather before him.

The Robson Transport headquarters was situated on a local industrial estate on the other side of town to the small farm cottage which was the base to the whole transport operations. Although it was a small-town business, David Robson had really pulled out all of the stops to get into every area. The company's vehicle fleet included everything from a lightning-fast Honda CB650 Nighthawk motorcycle designed for local and small London deliveries right up to a forty-tonne articulated Scania P94D for long runs and overweight loads. David Robson's business mind-set of 'no job too big or small' was that of the legendary truck company Eddie Stobart. He was determined to get there regardless of the challenge, whether it was heavy snow or scorching heat. His life motto had been that of the Special Air Service: 'Who dares wins'. This had caused disagreements from time to time within the company and in the family, but then again, whoever had heard of a family or a successful business that never argued or disagreed on anything?

A few weeks later, once Stuart had managed to get the specially modified racing wheels back on the BMW, he borrowed a small car transporter trailer from David. Under the cover of darkness, to make sure he wasn't being followed, he moved the BMW into one of the grey warehouse units at the head office buildings on the other side of town. The big question to everyone in the family was what he was doing all the time. Stuart hadn't told anyone about buying the car but had already managed to completely strip down and rebuild it with the exception of just one thing. He always had the ambition of fitting a very powerful engine to the BMW. But it had taken a lot of modifications, including reconfiguring the entire gearbox and clutch plate so that it would be able to take the power of the new engine.

The sun had started to set across the country as Stuart polished the last fitted piece of the new engine, which was mounted on an engine stand in a corner of the small warehouse unit. Throwing a black cover sheet over the now-completed engine, he stretched and dropped the old bit of rag on the work bench before walking straight towards the small door in another corner, switching the lights out as he went. When he pulled up in front of the farmhouse ten minutes later on his black Harley Davidson motorcycle, he found a light on in the window. Everybody was still up even though it was well past eleven at night. Dismounting the motorcycle, he wheeled it into the barn and locked the doors before walking back across the yard and letting himself into the house.

Stuart went to bed that night not worried about getting up early in the morning, as he had the next day off as paid holiday. That night he fell asleep very quickly but soon wished he hadn't. From a neurotypical or non-autistic perspective, seeing a woman dressed in white would be a sign of great happiness. It put him in mind of beautiful brides on their wedding day waiting to be walked up the aisle. Now and for the second time in a few months the angel had reappeared again, this time a little closer to him, with her shoulder-length brown hair blowing around as if in the wind. Stuart was staring right at her this time, not ashamed as to the nature of the dream but eager to find out more of why she was there and what it meant.

He looked down at his feet and found that he was wearing the thick black flying boots he had once owned when he was a pilot in the air corps. When he looked back up he suddenly jumped with shock; the brown-haired woman had glided forward until she and Stuart were nose to nose.

'Who are you?' asked Stuart. He stood his ground, feeling the hairs on his arms standing on end as they always did when someone of the opposite sex came within what was called 'social limitation'. He couldn't think of what to do. She was leaning in closer. Her body heat radiated so much that Stuart felt like he was burning up from the inside. Terrified, he felt his knees give way. He collapsed to the floor and crawled away as fast as he could with the brown-haired woman still advancing on him.

She obviously wanted something from him because she didn't seem to want to let him wake up. Stuart shut his eyes tight and threw his hands up over his face, waiting for the blow to fall. It didn't come. He opened his eyes slowly and saw that the brown-haired woman wasn't attacking him at all. Instead, she was holding out her hand as if to help Stuart to his feet. Stuart was confused; at first he thought that she only wished to attack him, as his senses were so regularly on high alert when he came within breathing distance of the opposite sex. After a pause of a few seconds he picked himself up and grabbed hold of her hand. There was a sharp pull as she hoisted him up with some strength and agility, breathing very gently. It seemed she was strong as well as attractive.

They were nose to nose now, looking into each other's faces. He felt her hand moving around his neck and then a slight tug as she pulled his military dog tags up from around his neck. He hoped that she wasn't about to rip them from around his neck. Stuart was very attached to them, having been allowed to keep them after leaving the Air Training Corps as a teenager. It brought back memories of his days as a simulator fighter pilot, which had been some of the best years of his life. She seemed to study them for a second before letting them drop back down behind his T-shirt. Stuart looked up just in time to see that her eyes were a dark brown colour, exactly the same colour as his were. He wasn't remotely scarred of her anymore but still seemed hypnotised by the look she was giving him.

Even though fear of the opposite sex was standard procedure with all on the autistic spectrum, the angel still seemed to have a very powerful air around her. This kept Stuart where he was even though every muscle in his body was telling him to run as fast as he could in the other direction. As suddenly as it had started, everything stopped. The brown-haired woman backed away from him before fading into smoke, and Stuart was brought crashing back to reality. He sat bolt upright in bed, sweat running all over him, and really felt as though he had just been in close company with the brown-haired woman in his dream. *I don't know why I called you the angel. The way you move is almost like a ghost,* thought Stuart, finally clearing his head and finding that the feeling of weightlessness had left him.

'Mind box,' said Stuart, having the sudden thought that maybe these visions of the brown-haired woman were his brain's way of cleaning itself. It did get so bunged up these days with information and feelings. Turning over, he saw that the bedside clock only read four minutes past five in the morning. Feeling that falling asleep again would be an absolute no-no, he pulled himself up and begun to get dressed ready for a day's holiday down at the warehouse finishing off the BMW's final stages. He did not know that this particular day would change his life forever.

Chapter Five

Love at First Sight

Emily Green was, you might say, your outstanding university graduate: highly intelligent, very attractive, and, most importantly of all, always wanting to have a good time with her extensively long list of friends. She also just happened to be chairwomen of the student union at her university, which placed her at a very respectable position within the graduate community. Emily had recently returned home from the American state of Alabama, where she had taken a gap year from university. She lived at home with her parents back in the same town as Stuart in Hertfordshire. It was a fine house hand built from aged Tudor oak, making it look more like an old-fashioned village pub. It was definitely on a much grander scale than the Robson family's out-of-town farmhouse.

Emily herself was around five foot, nine inches tall. She had shoulder-length blonde hair and a great love of her golden retriever, Trixie. When she wasn't being buried under by all of her university work, Emily's favourite hobby was the same as Stuart's: driving. Although she had never let on to her friends in the past about her love of driving, pretending to have a love of fashion instead, she would often dream of owning what her mum called a footballer's car. Her greatest ambition was to own one of the high-end Aston Martin DB series cars, with their V12 supercharged engines and six-figure price tags. But for the time being she would have to settle for her present car: a 55-plate, 1.3-litre midnight-black Ford Fiesta.

Emily was lying on her bed, curled up with her favourite novel, when she was suddenly interrupted by a tap on the door. 'Emily, I'm heading out to see a friend of mine. Want to come for the ride?' came the voice of her father, Rick Green, from the other side of the door.

'Okay, I'll be there in a second,' said Emily as she heard her father's footsteps walking away back down the stairs. Closing her book, she placed it on her bedside table before grabbing her jacket from the chair in the corner and exiting her bedroom. She found her father already in the car when she reached the front door a few minutes later. A crystal white 4x4 Volvo XC60 gleamed brightly in the morning sunshine. In practicality, it was nearer to a NASA space shuttle than a car in terms of technology and gadgets compared to other vehicles.

After a five-minute drive or so, the white Volvo pulled up in the car park of the small industrial estate where the sign 'Robson Transport Limited' hung above the gateway into the yard. David was sitting in his office, as he usually did on his Friday morning shift. Out in the yard two forklift trucks drove backwards and forwards from the warehouse, bringing pallets out and loading them onto the double-decked, tri-axle articulated trailer hitched up to a Scania lorry. On seeing them out of the window, David got up from his desk and made his way outside to greet Rick and Emily, who had both got out and walked towards the office building. Emily, meanwhile, had been a bit distracted by a sudden flash of white paintwork, which had come from out of an open doorway opposite to the site office.

Intrigued by this sudden flash, she slowly walked round the corner and was immediately brought back to her senses. 'Feel free to have a look around, Emily. I don't mind,' said David as she nodded in his direction, jumping slightly at the sudden gesture. As David and Rick disappeared into the office building, she made her way inside the warehouse unit, where she was greeted by an awesome sight. Propped up on some vehicle trolley jacks was the newly completed BMW race car 'Thunderbolt'. Emily's eyes lit up with delight as she saw what was sitting in front of her. There was a sudden noise to her right as she spun round to look. There was no-one there, but Emily could have sworn she saw a figure in the corner of her eye. She quickly returned her gaze back to Thunderbolt and started to run her hand along the bodywork.

The small noise sounded again, only this time Emily didn't have time to respond as a shadow loomed behind her. She felt a lump come to her throat as she slowly turned around to find Stuart standing there with a spanner in his hand and a look of amazement on his face. Emily gave out a small scream at the shock of seeing him standing there but soon relaxed a little, realizing he must have been one of the yard staff.

'Sorry, I didn't mean to intrude. The door was open, and nobody was in. I spotted this amazing race car here and wanted to have a look,' said Emily, stuttering slightly at the shock of seeing Stuart standing there. To her complete and utter surprise, Stuart didn't answer straight away but instead stood quite close and looked down at her.

At this point Emily felt a little intimidated, as he was a lot bigger than her and was much more well-built. Stuart suddenly backed down and placed the spanner on the floor. 'Please do not fear me. I mean you no harm,' said Stuart, almost like a robot relaying an instruction to its operator.

'I'm not scared,' said Emily as she relaxed a little bit. She had a sudden image of Hagrid from the Harry Potter novels: big and powerful but at the same time friendly and often mistaken for a man made of stone. Emily was still looking at Stuart from behind her sunglasses, but she quickly took them off when she realised why everything seemed to be so dark inside. It was at that moment Stuart felt weak at the knees, and a sudden urge came over him as though an invisible aid were helping him along.

His whole sensual systems had frozen in one go. For the first time in his life he felt a powerful surge through his body which should have been telling him to run. But this time it was different; he felt warm and peaceful and even had a small feeling of a cramp stomach. Fright was always on the surface of his mind every time there was a member of the opposite sex on the scene, but now it seemed that this was just a distant memory.

For the first time in ages, Emily had the impression that she was not being looked at in a sexual way but in a loving and caring way. 'Are you an angel?' asked Stuart after looking Emily up and down for a second or so.

'Sorry,' she said, smiling slightly as she had the courage to look up slightly straight into Stuart's eyes.

'An angel. I hear some of the really cool racing drivers have them. They say it brings them good luck before each race. They're said to be some of the most attractive girls anywhere,' said Stuart. He picked up his spanner again from the floor and walked towards Emily, fixing it onto the mounting bolts holding the engine to the frame.

Emily seemed a bit taken aback at this point but thought carefully about this sudden statement. 'I don't know any racing drivers in person. What are you trying to do, anyway?' asked Emily, leaning up against the BMW before looking down into the engine bay.

At this point Stuart would often be saying to people 'Don't lean on the car,' but for some reason he didn't seem to mind her doing it. At last he had found someone who spoke his language. Excitement started to grow in him.

'It's complicated mechanical parts. You wouldn't understand it,' said Stuart.

Emily's eyes widened a little bit. 'I do like cars, you know. I don't just spend my whole day brushing my hair and choosing what to wear,' said Emily, a little put out at Stuart's tone of voice.

Stuart recoiled a little at Emily's sudden outburst but realised that there was a different air about her than all the other ladies that he'd ever met. 'I've just mounted the modified V10 engine to the frame; I've had to reinforce the sub-frame so that the vibration of the engine doesn't shake itself loose from its mounting bolts,' explained Stuart almost as confidently as a university lecturer would address a hall full of eager looking students having a debate.

Whilst Stuart had been explaining this, Emily had been taking it all in. Her attention focused down into the engine bay, checking out the clutch unit, the gear box, and the newly fitted turbo chargers as well as the Audi sports nine hundred horsepower V10 engine. But it seemed like she had done it completely by accident. She had got Stuart onto his favourite specialised subject. Stuart was off like a shot, talking over all of the modifications he had done along with the repainted chassis, the bodywork, and the big wing spoiler mounted on the rear of the car, which was well over six feet in length and stood at least eight inches high, covering enough of the car's rear end to keep it down on the road when in a race.

By this time Stuart had been talking quite swiftly for at least a good ten minutes. Emily stood beside him, thinking that she might have met someone who took their hobby a little more seriously than she did. When he had finished talking Emily looked at him a little wide-eyed. She had a slight smile but not her usual broad grin.

'Wow, you really know your stuff,' said Emily, choosing her words carefully, as Stuart hadn't taken a breath once in his explanation.

'Are you okay?' said Stuart so suddenly that Emily was caught unawares.

'Yes, I'm fine,' said Emily abruptly. She seemed to be a bit confused. *Why has he suddenly asked me that? I've been okay all this time,* thought Emily as she realised that Stuart was still looking at her.

Only standing in at around five feet nine inches tall, she found it a bit difficult to look directly into Stuart's eyes, but she did make an effort. 'Why are you looking at me like that?' said Emily, not in an offended voice but a curious one instead.

'I was –' said Stuart, but he broke off quickly as Emily grinned again.

'Was what'? she said in that curious voice again, flicking her hair back behind her ear.

'I was just … admiring your figure,' said Stuart. He paused slightly, thinking what to say next, as Emily relaxed a little. She thought him slightly odd to start off with, but it seemed that was his strange way of paying her a compliment.

'Are you saying I've got a nice body?' said Emily. Stuart felt his ears start to heat up, which was always a sign to him that he was getting very uncomfortable with the situation.

Where's your own mother when you need her? thought Stuart. She was the best person to have at hand in these sorts of situations. It was usually at this point that all of his systems in his head, including the powerful mind box, would kick in and give him a swift answer to his problem. But in the here and now it would have been no good for a number of reasons. Firstly, he wasn't in a safe environment to activate it. Secondly, Emily may have thought there was something strange going on if he closed his eyes right in front of her.

'Yes I do,' said Stuart so suddenly he took himself by surprise. At this point Emily let out a small giggle. She raised a hand to her mouth to quickly stifle it.

'What's so funny? I don't understand,' said Stuart, confused all over.

'Has anyone ever told you that you're really weird?' said Emily, trying not to sound insulting.

'But I don't understand. My mother always told me that girls like to be made to feel good about themselves,' said Stuart as Emily smiled again.

'Yes, but that's usually when you're on a date; not when you've only just met each other for the first time,' said Emily in a voice which sounded like she was trying to explain to someone that one plus one equalled two.

'Are you asking me on a date?' said Stuart, sounding really surprised. Emily suddenly turned away to look at something on the wall, but for the tiniest of seconds Stuart could have sworn he'd seen her go bright red. Turning back, she was about to answer Stuart's question when David and Rick walked around the open shutter doorway.

'That's great, Rick. I'll have those timber sections picked up and moved within the week,' said David as he spotted Stuart and Emily together.

'There you are. I wondered where you'd got to,' said Rick, looking at Emily standing next to Stuart.

'It's all right, Dad. I was just coming,' said Emily as she turned to walk back towards the doorway, realising that she'd left Stuart hanging on the question he'd just asked of her.

'Oh, you've never met before. Rick, this is my eldest son, Stuart,' said David to cut the awkward silence that had come up between the four of them.

'Very pleased to meet you, sir,' said Stuart, walking forward to shake Rick's hand before realising that his hands were still dirty from where he had been fitting the engine mounting bolts. To his surprise Rick took his hand and shook it without waiting for him to clean it.

'Don't worry, Stuart. I do like someone who doesn't mind getting his hands dirty on things. I see you've already met my daughter, Emily,' said Rick, giving Emily a little squeeze on the shoulder.

'Yes, I caught her eyeing up Thunderbolt while you and my dad were discussing business,' said Stuart as Rick laughed.

'She loves her cars – been a big fan of *Top Gear* since she was eleven years old, bless her,' said Rick as Emily went slightly pink.

'Aww, don't embarrass me, Dad,' she said, smiling slightly and pulling out some keys from her pocket.

'Ah, I do believe my taxi service is waiting. Good to see you again, David. Pleasure to meet you, Stuart,' said Rick as he and Emily walked away across the yard towards a white Volvo XC60 4x4 which was parked up in front of the main office building.

'Emily. I like that name,' said Stuart as he and David watched the white Volvo drive away out of the main gate.

'Okay, out with it,' said David as the two of them walked back through the open shutter door.

'Out with what? Nothing happened,' said Stuart, reopening the bonnet on Thunderbolt and finishing off the work he had started.

'Stu, don't try and kid me. I wasn't born yesterday,' said David. A slight grin appeared on his face as he leaned up against the side of Thunderbolt.

'I still don't get it. What is it that you're trying to get at?' said Stuart, still with his head under the bonnet.

'You're in love with Emily Green,' said David.

Stuart reacted so quickly he banged his head against the open bonnet. Giving a sharp cry of pain, he retracted his head out from under the bonnet and looked David square in the face. 'I'm not in love with her. That's the curse of having Asperger's; we don't get to fall in love,' exclaimed Stuart, rubbing the back of his head where he had hit it on the bonnet.

'Stuart, I'm no doctor. But I could see your pupils had dilated, your heart looked like it was about to come out of your chest, and you're shaking like a rake,' said David as Stuart instinctively looked down at his hand. David was right. His right hand had started to shake so much that it looked ready to fall off.

'I felt exactly the same way about your mother when I first met her. It's the whole love at first sight thing,' said David.

'But I don't want a girlfriend. And anyway, she even said herself she thought I was weird,' said Stuart.

'She probably said that because she's never met anyone like you before and she doesn't know what to think,' replied David in a reassuring sort of way. 'Just have a think about it. This could be the start of something new. Maybe she could be your next best friend.' David gave Stuart a little tap on the shoulder before standing up and walking out of the shutter door, leaving Stuart to his thoughts.

'But we don't have friends,' said Stuart to himself, giving Thunderbolt a small tap before heading back towards his toolbox. By the time Stuart had finished fitting the last upgraded features, the sun had started to set on the horizon, so he decided to call it a night. Grabbing his crash helmet, he headed out of the shutter, closing the door behind him and making sure all of the security alarms were set before he left. That day had left him with something of a puzzling mystery. Why had it affected him that much? What was different? What changed, and why?

Chapter Six

Doorstep Small Talk

Stuart returned home that night with a plan clearly formulated in his head. He had to know more about Emily. Who was she, and why had she affected him like that? It seemed strange. In most cases he passed by everyone not looking twice at them, whether they were of the opposite sex or not. *Maybe this is what I've been overlooking, the missing link into becoming more like everyone else, like a human being,* he would often think to himself as he lay there trying to fall asleep every night.

For the next couple of days Stuart looked everywhere he could for advice on going on dates. There was plenty of information, from books at his local library to professional advice on the Internet, but this was for 'normal people', not for Aspies with a fear of the opposite sex and those who had never have been on a date in their life.

When Stuart approached the librarian stacking the shelves and asked her, in his words, about 'dating for autism', she said he was in the wrong place and should be making a doctor's appointment at the local hospital instead. After days of going through everything he could find, there was only one avenue left to explore. He had been a little shaken by his encounter with Emily for the first time and had been trying to pluck up the courage to go round to her house and ask her for help. In the days that followed David had looked at Stuart with small grin on his face but realised that pushing his eldest son too far would cause him to have a mental overload and shut everyone out.

It was only when Stuart woke up one Saturday morning a few weeks after his first encounter with Emily that he decided that he would have to be brave and just go for it. Under the cover of running his Harley Davidson motorcycle out for its usual weekend run, as it was a nice, sunny morning, Stuart headed straight across town to Emily's house. Parking the Harley round the corner, he felt a slight shiver go down his back, as if fear itself were creeping just behind the hedge in front of him. Swallowing hard, he marched straight up the over-packed driveway – Rick and his family owned a number of very nice cars – and rapped smartly on the front door. As he stood there, arms behind his back, he took in the numerous cars, which included a midnight-black 2005 Ford Mustang muscle car complete with white racing stripes.

'Five-litre V8 with a sports air intake and racing spoiler wing. Very impressive,' said Stuart to himself, taking in the high-end five-figure motor, which had a gleam about it due to the morning sunshine. Without warning the door was suddenly flung open so quickly that Stuart jumped backwards and nearly fell over the wheel of the Mustang parked next to him. Stopping himself quickly, he looked back up and nearly froze as for a second he thought Emily herself was standing there in the doorway. On closer inspection it wasn't Emily, but the woman standing before him had a very similar look. This woman's name was Julie Green. Process of elimination quickly let Stuart work out that she had to be Emily's mother. She was around the same height as Emily was but with shoulder-length brown hair instead of the blonde highlights that Emily had.

'Good morning. Can I help you?' said Julie as she took in Stuart's cowboy boots and classic motorcycle leather jacket.

Stuart had decided that the best approach was to put on a voice that he usually did as a common party trick. 'Good morning, madam; my name is Robson. I was wondering if it was possible to speak to Miss Emily – if it's of no inconvenience, of course,' said Stuart in his very convincing bumbling Englishman accent.

'One moment, please; I'll see if she's available,' said Julie, looking a little confused at this sudden request.

'Thank you, ma'am,' replied Stuart as Julie retracted her head back inside the house, leaving Stuart alone again outside admiring the midnight black Ford Mustang.

'Oh hi, it's you,' said a familiar voice. Stuart turned around to look at Emily Green herself directly in the eye. Like before, Emily had the effect of making Stuart feel tense and uptight. And then it started again like it had at the warehouse. Stuart felt that tingling up his spine and the feeling that his whole brain was defenceless against an attack of a nature he'd never known before in his life. Emily had that smile on her face that he would recognise anywhere. It seemed that his focus may have gone out of line very slightly. The next thing he knew, Emily was waving a hand in front of him.

'Hello,' she was saying, wondering what was happening. As soon and sudden as it started, it all just stopped dead; his brain was back to normal, and his eyes had come back into focus.

His spine was still shivering a little bit, but now he was left with an awkward silence between himself and Emily, who by this time was thinking that this was some sort of practical prank her friends had cooked up.

'Sorry about that. Must have been a bit tired,' said Stuart, thinking quickly at the situation.

'You do look a bit tired,' said Emily in her usual soft voice. She was right, of course. He'd had another one of his dreams again the previous night, which as usual involved the one thing he feared above all others.

'Yer, tell me about it; you get so attached to your job it means you don't realise you're getting tired,' said Stuart, thinking up a reason to explain why he had just blacked out like that. It had never happened when he was around anyone else – especially not when he was driving, which was good news – so why had it happened now?

'What do you do for a living?' asked Emily, sounding quite interested.

'I drive vans delivering bathroom equipment all over the country,' replied Stuart, still feeling the chills on his spine.

'Really? That sounds cool. I always thought you worked for your dad,' said Emily.

'I did try that one when I left school, but my dad refused to employ me. He'd started from nothing and made his way up, and he wanted me to do the same,' said Stuart, talking normally now. He couldn't believe he'd been in Emily's presence for over twenty minutes now, and apart from the sudden mental block at the start, the chat seemed to be going really well.

'So what brings you here? You can't be here just for the fun of it,' said Emily. Stuart looked a bit sheepish.

'What's up?' said Emily, who had not failed to notice this change in Stuart's expression.

'I came here to ask you something,' said Stuart. He felt a slight surge of confidence, almost as if an invisible force were egging him on.

Emily's eyes widened in surprise but soon returned to normal as she replied, 'Really? What's that?'

'Will you go out with me?' said Stuart so quickly the words went garbled as he spoke them.

'Sorry?' said Emily in a surprised voice. But like before, she seemed to display one of those girlish grins for the smallest of seconds.

'I want to ask you out on a date. I feel that I'm completely hopeless and isolated in the world of relationships, and I am asking you very nicely if you can help me,' said Stuart a little more slowly this time.

Emily didn't answer straight away. She seemed to be taking Stuart in for a minute or so before giving a response. It almost seemed like she was trying to avoid something herself. 'Ahh, that's so sweet. You don't sound like a creep to me, so I'll say yes,' said Emily as Stuart's heart gave a little jolt.

'Yes? Is that yes, you will help me, or a yes to something else?' said Stuart feeling his face muscles ache as he started to smile for the first time in what felt like years.

'Yes to the "I'll help you with your dating problem" bit,' said Emily, flicking her hair back behind her ear.

'Thank you,' said Stuart. As he did so he moved himself forward and outstretched his arms in order to give Emily a hug.

'Wow, what are you doing?' said Emily, suddenly backing away and sticking her hands up in shock.

'Sorry, bit carried away,' said Stuart, suddenly retreating backwards as if Emily had suddenly waved a hot poker at him.

'Usually in terms of relationships the hugs and physical things come later,' said Emily.

'Please forgive me, Miss Green. I did not mean to frighten you,' said Stuart as Emily relaxed a little, giving another small smile.

'Emily, darling, lunch is ready,' came the sound of Julie's voice from inside the house.

'Coming, Mum,' said Emily before turning back to Stuart.

'Duty calls,' said Stuart in a jokey sort of voice.

'Yer, I suppose so,' said Emily as Stuart pulled out a scrap piece of paper which he had written his phone number on earlier that day.

'If you ever want meet up sometime,' said Stuart, handing the piece of paper over to Emily.

'Thanks,' she said, taking it and putting it in her pocket. Stuart froze for a second because he couldn't think what to say.

Instead he just gave a little wave with his left hand as Emily smiled again and closed the door. Stuart turned away, still not believing his luck. Emily had agreed to help him. His insides seemed to be doing cartwheels. *Beautiful day, isn't it?* thought Stuart to himself as he strode back down the driveway around to where he had parked his Harley motorcycle. Swinging himself back over the bike, he kicked it into life and slid his crash helmet back over his head. With a clunk from the heavy built gearbox, he pulled away towards the main road, which took him back out of town towards home. He rolled up the lane into the yard and noticed a familiar white Yamaha XJ6 sports bike parked next to the farmhouse. This motorbike belonged to his one true all-time favourite best friend, Ben Spencer.

Chapter Seven

Motorcycle Trails

Ben was one of those friends with whom nothing was a problem. Having got Stuart into cars and bikes whilst being at school together, every time it was a brilliant, clear, sunny day Ben would suggest a ride on their bikes through the countryside. Ben would always beat him because the Yamaha XJ6 was clearly the best bike for speed and handling. Stuart's own beloved Harley Davidson was more of a cruiser, although that didn't stop him from chucking it around a bit. Dismounting his bike and leaning it on its side stand, Stuart made for the house. As he opened the front door, he heard the sound of Ben's voice coming from the front living room.

'Benny boy,' called out Stuart in a friendly voice. He came round the doorway to find him and Abigail sitting in armchairs, each holding a cup of tea.

'Stu, I've been waiting for you,' said Ben, jumping up and shaking Stuart's hand.

'I guess you want a ride out. I've been just running the Harley in myself,' said Stuart as Ben nodded his head in earnest, rubbing his hands in anticipation.

'I'll let you boys have fun, but be back in time for dinner, Stu,' said Abigail. She handed over a cup of tea for Stuart, who drank it in one go and placed it back in her hand.

'Thanks, Mum,' said Stuart, giving her a huge hug and turning to leave with Ben.

'Stu, are you okay?' asked Abigail, noticing the broad grin spreading across his face.

'Never better,' said Stuart. Ben tapped him on the shoulder as the pair of them headed out into the yard.

It was typical for the both of them to go travelling on their bikes to all areas of the country. So far they had been to East Anglia, Kent, and the Home Counties. Once, over a five-day period, they went down to the well-known tourist attraction known as Land's End in the large landscape county of Cornwall.

'Where are we going this time?' asked Ben as Stuart picked up his crash helmet and went to slide it onto his head.

'I chose last time. It's your turn, mate.' said Stuart.

Ben had a road map propped open on his fuel tank. This was right, of course; the last time they had gone on a road trip, Stuart had chosen the extraordinary area of natural beauty called the New Forest in Hampshire. This had been quite a memorable trip; Ben had seen his all-time favourite car, the Aston Martin Vanquish driven in the 2002 James Bond film *Die Another Day*, at the classic Motor Museum at Beaulieu.

'All right then, I've got the route planned out. Let's go,' said Ben before Stuart could get a look.

'A mystery tour. I like it,' said Stuart as he swung himself over the Harley, pushing the helmet down over his head. There was a roar from the Yamaha's 600cc engine. Stuart followed suit, kicking the Harley into life before moving forward after Ben down the lane towards the main road. Out on the main road, Ben opened up his throttle and soon put a big lead on Stuart. Soon, realising that he was going really fast, Ben slowed down so that Stuart could draw level with him. With the town far behind them, they headed into the countryside, first on a duel carriageway, and then onto the twisty country roads where hedgerows grew six and seven feet high before opening out into fields.

By the time they pulled up in a layby on top of a hill, they were looking down at the port of Harwich in Essex. From their viewpoint on the outskirts of the village of Ramsey they could see the ships coming in and out of the port bringing in all kind of freight, which were loaded onto trains and trucks before being delivered all over the country.

'Look at that view,' said Ben when the two of them had sat down on a bench outside a roadside café overlooking the port. The Yamaha and the Harley Davidson motorcycles stood only feet away, gleaming in all their glory in the bright sunshine.

'Yes,' said Stuart, not really sounding himself. He stared out to sea at the massive container ship, which was coming into the port. Ben turned to look at him but soon noticed the dilated pupils and the faint grin, which could only mean one thing.

Having been in the same situation as Stuart, Ben had never had a girlfriend himself, but that wasn't through trying. He would often joke and say that his face would smash mirrors even if he wasn't looking into them. Stuart always replied that Ben wasn't ugly at all; he just hadn't found the right person yet.

'I didn't say anything back there, you know. I'll let you tell your parents when you're ready,' said Ben as Stuart looked at him, a little confused.

'You may be my greatest friend, Ben, but you do confuse me sometimes,' said Stuart, taking a swig from the can of Diet Coke he was holding.

'You've got the bug,' said Ben with a broad grin on his face.

'Sorry, Ben. I think you're confused a bit. I don't own a Volkswagen Beetle, although it sounds like an ideal restoration project,' said Stuart, taking another swig.

'I wasn't talking about that sort of bug; I was talking about the one where you've met someone you fancy,' said Ben as Stuart almost choked on his drink in shock.

'You as well? I must have the word "Idiot" tattooed on my forehead or something. Why do people have this thing about me being in love with her?' said Stuart, a little put out by everyone's assumption of his situation. In truth that was the case; from the perspective of a non-autistic, the symptoms of love were clear. It seemed that the only person who couldn't see that was Stuart himself. He seemed to have encountered something that was like nothing he remembered.

'I don't know what to do. My heart is telling me to go full steam ahead, but my brain is suffering some sort of mental overload,' said Stuart.

Ben looked at him, thinking hard himself on what to do next. He couldn't really give Stuart any advice, but having a friendly face at hand was always one comfort. 'Just go for it. I mean, what's the worst that could happen? She says no,' said Ben as Stuart turned to look at him.

'That's just the thing, Ben. What happens if my brain won't take that sort of rejection full on?' replied Stuart in an attempt to find a counterargument for his situation.

'Only time will tell, my good friend,' said Ben as Stuart grinned and clapped him on the shoulder. They both stared into the horizon, looking down into the Harwich port as another huge container ship laden with more goods bound for all over the United Kingdom sailed slowly into the port towards the army of cranes waiting to offload it.

They watched the sun slowly sink in the sky, talking about all sorts of things, from the latest news around the world to the maiden test runs of Thunderbolt, until Ben openly yawned and suggested they should be getting back. Stuart arrived home around an hour later to find the farm yard in complete darkness with no lights on in any of the house windows. He quietly let himself in, knowing that he was going to be up early in the morning for a track day at Rockingham racetrack. But it seemed that the night had another instalment waiting for him. He finally drifted off only after lying awake in bed for an hour or so thinking things over in his mind. Emily's face swam around in his mind's eye, not taunting him as such but almost seeming like the ghost of someone he had wronged.

Emily's face faded into blackness as Stuart drifted into an easy doze, but this was soon to be something of another mystery wrapped up in an enigma. He dreamed he was standing up in the middle of a stage inside a massive theatre. It was dark, but he could tell that every seat was filled with a keen-eared listener. Looking down, he could see he was wearing an office suit and tie with a nametag on his blazer which read 'Doctor Stuart Robson'. The crowd were silent as a voice came over the megaphone like the voice of a continuity announcer: 'Ladies and Gentlemen, may we present Doctor Stuart Robson of Oxford University.' The crowd applauded its approval and then fell silent a minute later as instinctively Stuart begun talking as if he did this every day.

Behind him, resting on a highly polished stand lit up by a single stage spotlight, was the over-super-modified Audi V10 engine which usually sat inside the touring race car Thunderbolt. As he talked his life away, giving his lecture to the crowd of many interested faces, Stuart's attention was suddenly drawn towards the back of the theatre, where a balcony hung above the back seats overlooking the stage. Just visible in and around all of the stage lighting and background effects was the brown-haired angel Stuart had come to see more and more often in the last couple of weeks. Her outline was a pale white again, almost like a ghost. Before he could stop to think about what he was doing, Stuart had launched himself off the stage. He landed smartly on his feet and started to sprint the length of the theatre to catch this mystery angel before she disappeared again.

Without warning the ground beneath his feet suddenly changed from carpet to green grass, and a sudden explosion behind him made Stuart hit the deck. Grass and dirt flew twenty feet into the air as another explosion went off only a few yards to his left. He realised he was under fire from some unknown hostile force. Most people at this point would be frightened out of their minds at this level of intensity. This sort of situation for Stuart, however, was almost a daily occurrence; he often had the feeling that his whole world was in chaos and disarray. Where most people would see a perfectly normal environment, such as a nightclub or wedding, sufferers of autism found an active warzone.

As Stuart lay there keeping his eyes fixed on the angel in the background, a whole cloud of grass and dirt rained down on top of him. Another explosion went off right next to him. The angel was only fifty or so feet away, but she was standing upright rather than diving for cover. *That just proves it; you have to be a ghost*, thought Stuart to himself. Even the bravest of people wouldn't stand upright in the middle of a bombardment. But before he had the chance to make his next move, a loud whistling sound was cutting through the air. He realised too late that he was right in the line of fire. The shell landed right where he lay. Stuart sat bolt upright in bed with sweat running down his face, as it always did after these dreams.

Bringing his breathing under control, Stuart reached across to his bedside table and took a mouthful of water from the jug he always kept by his bed. Coming prepared was something Stuart prided himself on. His favourite saying was that of Hannibal Smith from the A-Team: 'I love it when a plan comes together'. Having taken a gulp of water, he lay his head back on his pillows and ran a hand through his hair, thinking back to his vision of the angel. More questions seem to come up in his mind rather than useful answers. Having a sudden thought, Stuart closed his eyes and fired up his well-known mind box system. Once inside he started to construct what was known as the mind map, placing bits of information up on a wall-sized pin board in front of him like a police team would when investigating a major crime.

After a couple of minutes he opened his eyes again, having constructed his mental mind map to find that he had drawn a big blank. According to his overwhelming logic the angel must be a trick of the light or even a figment of his overstretched imagination. Realising it was a complete loss, Stuart rolled over and tried to get back to sleep, putting the vision of the angel to the back of his already overcrowded mind. Now he came to think of it, every single vision that he had witnessed over the last couple of months had featured her somewhere within it, so she had to mean something. But if that was the case, why didn't she ever speak to him or even try to help him instead of just staring at him like some long-forgotten friend? For Stuart, however, the future looked bright. Today was the day that would mean everything to him. Thunder was go.

Chapter Eight

Rockingham Shakedown

Sleep-deprived nights always led to groggy mornings. Stuart yawned over his bowl of porridge and listened to the rest of his family crashing about in the background, preparing for their busy day. David had insisted on coming with Stuart, as this was a very important day for the both of them. After months of preparing, repairing, modifying, and just experimenting around with different designs and products, it was now time for the moment of truth: the maiden test run of the mighty Thunderbolt itself. The heat of the porridge woke him up considerably. He pictured a cartoon character swallowing a chilli pepper and then watching the steam come venting out of its ears.

As Stuart opened the shutter door of the warehouse unit at Robson Transport HQ an hour later, he watched the sunlight hit the gleaming white bodywork of the trailer. Inside was Thunderbolt itself, strapped down with a number of ratchet straps and slings. For a bit of joke, and because Stuart was good at drawing, he had taken it on himself to paint a life-sized version of Thunderbolt on both sides of the trailer. This seemed to amuse most people; a few days earlier Ben had banged his nose on the side, thinking that it was a flatbed trailer and not a box one.

'Today's the day, old girl. Time for those mods to show what they can do,' said Stuart, banging his hand on the side of the trailer in excitement. Now was the moment to do his favourite pastime: racing.

Their destination for the first test run was to be Rockingham race circuit in Northamptonshire. It was a couple of hours' drive away for a classic 1969 Series 2A Land Rover, which was the towing vehicle of choice for this trip. But it would be good fun to bounce around, as they always did with it on road trips up and down the country.

'I'm going on ahead, Stu, to see if I can try and get a head start,' said David after they hitched up the trailer behind the Land Rover. This was valid, as Stuart had never seen his father push the Land Rover above 40 mph before.

'I'll meet you there,' said Stuart with a small wave. He tapped his hand on the side of the trailer as it pulled out of the warehouse unit towards the open road. Stuart himself closed down the warehouse before walking a short distance to where a high-roofed, sky blue Ford Transit sat.

This van on the outside looked just like a normal commercial vehicle, but on the inside it had been converted to carry all of the racing computers and speed gauges. At the front was a small mobile office which was used by each driver during a race as a resting area for when there was a changeover. All of the tools that were needed to service and repair Thunderbolt if it went wrong were stored in upright red containers. Being slightly OCD as well as autistic, Stuart kept certain tools in certain places, and they were all straight and highly polished. After an hour or so, Stuart caught David up in the Land Rover only a few miles outside of Rockingham raceway in the wide open area of the Northamptonshire countryside.

Pulling up at the security gate twenty minutes later, David stuck his head out the window to talk to the security guard, who had a cup of tea in hand. 'Morning. We're here for the test run, under the name of Robson,' said David as the guard checked his computer.

'David and Stuart Robson, pit hanger number eleven. Straight over at the gate ahead and carry on towards the main stands,' instructed the guard. David thanked him and moved along. Stuart followed in behind with the Transit as they both headed towards the pit lane. After an hour or so the two of them had both set up the equipment in the van and on Thunderbolt for reading all of information that they needed for entering any races. Stuart knew that all homemade racing machines had to undergo an inspection before being allowed to race.

'Let's get through the red tape today so we're all set for later,' said David, tapping Stuart on the shoulder as Stuart looked back at him.

'I can't wait to get Thunderbolt up and running. When are they letting us run round the track on our own for the test run?' asked Stuart.

'This afternoon, they said about half past one. We've got the whole track to ourselves for about half an hour, but everyone else is going to be watching,' said David.

Stuart looked down at his watch. It was only half past twelve. 'Perfect, just the time I need,' said Stuart with an air of excitement. He pulled on his overalls before sliding himself underneath Thunderbolt. David smiled to himself at the sight of his eldest son doing what he loved.

'I went to see her, you know,' came Stuart's voice from underneath the car.

'Saw who?' asked David in confusion, taken by surprise by this sudden statement.

'Emily Green,' said Stuart, sticking his head out from under the car.

'Oh right, Emily,' said David with a slight pause. His expression changed from surprise to confusion. Then the penny dropped as he understood what Stuart had said.

'Oh, okay, you mean Rick's eldest daughter, the one who was with him when he came in the other day,' said David.

'Yes, that's her,' said Stuart with a slight glint in his eye that David hadn't failed to notice.

'Stu, I don't like to be a stick in the mud here, but you've always insisted that you have a fear of girls. So why the sudden interest in a woman that you know nothing about?' asked David, sounding interested rather than patronising.

'I've got a hunch about her. I thought I felt something for a second when she was near me. But I must have imagined it, because it was there one second and gone the next,' replied Stuart in answer to David's question as he slid himself back underneath, taking a three-quarters AF-sized spanner with him.

'Silly question, but are you trying to unscrew the oil bolt under there?' said David, leaning down to Stuart's level.

'Yes. How did you know that?' said Stuart, sliding back out again and thinking hard at this last statement.

'Because the oil bolt size needs a fourteen-millimetre spanner to unscrew it; you're holding a three-quarters AF spanner,' said David, trying not to laugh.

'Ah,' said Stuart, looking at the spanner in his hand with surprise and a little amazement. Realising his mistake, he got up and swapped it over for the right spanner in the toolbox. David grinned to himself;

he liked seeing his son enjoying himself in this way. This was Stuart's sort of thing through and through.

As the day ticked by, Stuart and David watched the other cars fly past, going faster every time as they tried to beat their personal lap times. They saw every kind of car, from a nineteen-year-old boy racer in a tuned-up Vauxhall Corsa to a pensioner driving a scarlet-red Ferrari F50 supercar.

'It's time,' said Stuart excitedly at half past one on the dot. The other cars were all pulling themselves off of the track into the pit lane, making a path for Thunderbolt. Stuart proudly took the driver's seat for the first-ever test run of his very own, homemade touring car.

Picking up his helmet, Stuart slid it on over his head, lowering the microphone down to his mouth. He plugged the wire from the helmet into a small aux lead point on the centre consol. 'Radio check,' said Stuart, checking all of the on-board systems as he did so.

'Reading you loud and clear, Stu. Systems are up and running,' came David's voice through his headphones inside the crash helmet.

'Confirm all systems go for launch,' said Stuart in a jokey voice as David chuckled by the laptop he had open on the desk in front of him.

'Moment of truth, Stu; let's hear her sing,' said David. Stuart took a deep breath, inserted the main red starter key, and turned it clockwise. Then he found the green button on the centre console marked 'Start' and gave it a push.

A second passed before there was a spurt of fuel. The engine roared into life with a long, drawn-out revving of its newly built V10 supercharged beast of an engine.

'Yes!' said Stuart, punching the roof and instantly receiving a sharp pain to his hand. David was shaking his head in amazement at his son's brilliance to get Thunderbolt up and running. Then he started to cough due to the diesel smoke now filling the pit hanger as Stuart revved the engine.

'Smoke somewhere else, son. You're ruining a work of art,' said David. Stuart replied with an apology in a jokey sort of way before shooting out of the hanger onto the pit lane with a slight squeal of the tyres. Whilst in the pit lane there was a speed limit of 50 mph, which Stuart was up to in less than a second. He was soon on the slipway back onto the track.

'Show us what you've got, old girl,' said Stuart to himself as he pushed the accelerator pedal to the floor. Thunderbolt seemed to climb from a steady 50 to 80 mph in just a second. By the time he reached the first corner he was hard right hand down on the steering, feeling the back end of the car start to kick out. Stuart did what any racing driver dreamed about. Exiting the first corner, it was now time for another burst of speed. There was a squeal from the tyres as Thunderbolt left a cloud of white smoke in his wake. Stuart pushed the accelerator again, this time to 100 mph before the next corner, which went hard left into a hairpin.

'Leave me some tyre on the rim, won't you?' said David into his headset as Stuart laughed out loud.

'Ten four on that, Dad,' said Stuart as he came onto the finishing straight.

'Give her the beans, Stu; full power,' said David.

'Copy that. Engaging full power,' said Stuart, punching his foot hard to the floor. In the next instant he felt like he was flying a jet fighter rather than a driving a racing car; such was the force that took over when he hit the accelerator. Having exited the corner doing well over 70 mph he watched in the space of a few seconds the speedometer climb to 130 mph and kept climbing. His arms started to go numb as the cornering G-forces started to have an effect. When David radioed in to tell him that Thunderbolt had shot over the finish line at a recorded speed of over 186.8 mph, he was pleased beyond belief.

'I want to make 200 mph before the end of the test time,' said Stuart excitedly as he entered the first corner again, trying to beat his personal best speed record on the lap time. The other racing drivers in the pit lane cheered and clapped every time Thunderbolt passed them with a sudden gust of wind and a spectacular roar from the engine. It was like watching the Formula One cars charge past at the Grand Prix races.

'Come on, my turn now,' said David ten minutes later in a jokey voice to Stuart over the radio. On the side of the track the flag marshal had stepped out waving a chequered flag to tell Stuart to pull in and change driver.

'Coming in now, Dad,' said Stuart. He rolled into the pit lane and dropped his speed to 50 mph. Thunderbolt cruised to a stop outside the Team Robson pit.

Placing both hands on the inside of the framework, Stuart pulled himself out of the driver's seat as David stepped alongside him to take his place in the driver's seat.

'Go,' said Stuart in a jokey voice, waving his hand in front of him with a small bow. There was a squeal of tyres and a cloud of smoke as David punched his foot on the accelerator pedal, pushing Thunderbolt back out onto the circuit. Over the next half an hour or so David pushed Thunderbolt to its absolute limit, trying to get to that solid goal of 200 mph. But no matter how hard he tried, David just couldn't get the speed up.

'She will do two hundred; I know she will. I just can't understand why she's not,' said Stuart hours later back at home in the Robson farmhouse as he and David sat at the kitchen table drinking cups of tea.

'Don't be so hard on yourself, Stu. I do confess I'm not the fastest of drivers, so I don't think I would have got it up to that speed in just half an hour,' replied David as he drank his tea, pausing to think for a second about what could be done to solve the problem.

'Haven't you got your dinner thing with Emily Green tonight?' asked David all of a sudden as Stuart looked at his watch. He jumped a foot in the air when he saw what the time was.

'Yes I have, and I've only got forty-five minutes to go,' said Stuart. He started to tap his foot on the kitchen floor. His nerves were setting in again.

'You're going to be fine. Just remember the three rules of first dates: always compliment the dress, tell her she looks nice, and just, well, be yourself,' said David with a grin as Stuart's nerves did a backflip.

'Be myself? I can't even be sane for more than an hour at most around girls,' replied Stuart with a worried look on his face. David sighed and just went over to the sink to wash his cup up.

Stuart got up and made for the door out into the yard. 'I'll see you later,' said Stuart, feeling a lump start to come to his throat.

'Stuart,' said David as Stuart paused to look at him. 'We're proud of you, me and your mum,' said David in a reassuring voice, attempting to make Stuart less worried than he already was. Not being able to think of what to say at that moment in time, Stuart just grinned and exited to his waiting Harley Davidson motorcycle. Mounting himself on the saddle, he kicked it into life, and it roared away up the lane towards the town centre.

When he arrived at the public house known as The Rutland Hall a few minutes later the car park was almost empty, so he was spoilt for choice in terms of parking spaces. A few people looked up as the Harley cruised to a stop by some benches with its very distinct low, purring engine. Stuart dismounted and pulled off his crash helmet, slinging it into his rucksack before making his way inside. The small group looked on as Stuart entered the pub before looking back to the parked up Harley Davidson.

'That's a nice bike,' said one of them. His mates around him nodded in agreement. Inside the pub, however, Stuart approached the woman behind the bar, asking about the table he had booked a few days ago. She pointed him over to the one in the corner as he took his place, twisting his hands in his lap and trying to fight back his nerves.

Chapter Nine

The Idiot's Guide to Dating

Stuart tried to take his mind off his nerves through his annoying habit of straightening placemats along with knives and forks on the table in front of him. Suddenly there was the sound of an opening door. A sudden rush of cold air came in, and then the door closed again. There was the sound of heels on a stone floor, and then Stuart was taken aback to see what greeted him from behind the wall which separated the bar from the restaurant. It was Emily, but it didn't look like her at first. She seemed to have done something with her hair. As she turned the corner, the low setting sun outside the window caught it for a second, giving it an almost glowing look. She was wearing a knee-length, sky blue dress with four-inch heels, which brought her level to Stuart's height.

'Hi,' said Emily with a slight grin. Stuart jumped up from his chair so quickly he banged into the table, almost knocking his drink over but also at the same time causing a pain in the private areas.

'Hi,' said Stuart, trying to stop his eyes from watering from the pain.

'Are you all right?' said Emily in a caring voice as Stuart sat back down again.

'Yer, must be a bit taller than I thought I was,' said Stuart with a small laugh as Emily sat down in her chair.

'Are you ready to order?' said a voice to their right. They both looked up to see the waitress who had been behind the bar earlier now standing at their table with a notebook and pencil.

'Ham, egg, and some chips with a side order of onion rings, please,' said Stuart as the waitress scribbled in her notebook before turning to Emily.

'Cod and chips with a side order of vegetables, please,' said Emily, who hadn't looked at the menu but seemed to know what she was doing. The waitress finished scribbling and moved away towards the kitchen. Emily turned back to Stuart, who had started playing with his hands in his lap, as he always did when he was confronted with scary situations. Although most of his years of experience had been spent dealing with people who were nasty and spiteful, now he knew that this was a completely different situation.

'You like codfish, then,' said Stuart in what he hoped sounded like an interested tone, still feeling a little shaky.

'I like tradition. It's a very English dish. Why just ham and eggs for you?' said Emily with a slight smile in a confident voice, as if she did this sort of thing all the time.

'I like simplicity,' Stuart replied. He decided that this was the moment to give Emily the present that he had brought for her. It wasn't very big, but he had complete confidence in himself that this was going to go down quite well with her.

'I got you something; I thought you might like it,' said Stuart. He reached into his motorcycle jacket and pulled out a small bottle of perfume before pushing it across the table towards Emily. The bottle itself was only half the size as a can of coke, but that didn't stop Emily's face from lighting up.

'Aww, that's so sweet of you; thank you,' said Emily. She felt her face start to go a little red as she realised that she hadn't thought of that for him.

Operation Prince Charming is a go, thought Stuart as he started to feel his confidence come back to him.

While he thought this, Emily scooped the little bottle off the table and into her handbag on the floor next to her. Stuart, meanwhile, had gone straight for his rucksack behind him whilst Emily was preoccupied with doing up her handbag and pulled out a small book to quickly check a chapter near to the middle.

'What's that?' said Emily, who had finished with her handbag and turned back to face him.

'Oh, the *Idiot's Guide to Dating*, a handy guidebook for all first-time daters who need help navigating the social barrier of the female mind,' said Stuart, reading off of the front cover before handing it over to Emily for her to have a look.

'You don't need this; it will come naturally to you in time,' said Emily with a grin, handing the book back to him as he hid it back in his bag.

'I don't know,' said Stuart, looking a little worried.

'Okay, let's spin this one for a minute,' said Emily, pulling her chair in and sweeping her hair back behind her shoulders. For the smallest of seconds Stuart felt that pang of nerves again, like that invisible force in his mind was egging him on.

'I'm a single woman at a bar. Impress me,' said Emily, resting her head on her arms, which she'd propped up on the table in front of her.

Stuart thought the best approach in this situation was to use the art of imitation, almost as a child would learn from their parents. Resting his arms on the table, he mirrored Emily's pose as she batted her eyelids at him in an attempt to grab his full attention. It suddenly struck him at that very moment that she was actually quite attractive.

'Emm, you look nice,' said Stuart with a slight grin in an attempt to look appealing.

Running in the opposite direction would have been a better alternative, as he felt his sensitivity hitting the roof. Emily, meanwhile, had taken this last sentence quite well. She let her hair fall back in front of her face as she thought what to say next.

'Try making it a little more personal,' replied Emily in an encouraging voice as Stuart paused again.

'I personally think you look nice,' said Stuart after a second of so of silence. Emily gave a small snigger, which she quickly turned into a small sneeze. She felt her hands slide over her face in total embarrassment.

I really don't understand girls. Why have they got to be so, you know, different? thought Stuart, feeling as if this whole dating idea was a complete and utter waste of time which autistic people didn't do even if their lives depended on it.

After a few seconds she pulled them away to see Stuart still looking back at her in total confusion. His gut instinct had always told him that girls liked being told they looked beautiful. And yet here was the most stunningly attractive person he'd ever met looking back at him with almost fresh embarrassment at the situation.

'I don't understand. What did I say? What did I do?' said Stuart, now confused to the breaking point.

Emily lowered her hands away from her face, for at the sound of Stuart's voice she'd become almost sorry for him. Pulling herself together she thought, *Oh dear God, this man is rubbish at dating,* but she knew that she would never be able to say that out loud to him.

'You're a bit of a novice to dating, aren't you?' asked Emily in her calm voice, still trying to fight back tears of laughter.

'Yer, I should get a set of L-plates to show people I'm still learning: unqualified dating disaster monkey coming through,' said Stuart.

At this point Emily couldn't control herself. She let out a laugh that was so distorted that the couple at the next table looked up in alarm. 'We're trying to be on a date, not a hen night,' said Emily when she had finished giggling like mad, but her face had still gone tomato red from laughing so much.

When Emily next spoke, she seemed to have taken on the voice of an instructor but wasn't being too formal. 'Speaking from a female perspective, the best thing for us is to be made to feel special, being told we look nice, and just general kindness.'

'I do like your hair,' said Stuart, trying to think of what he liked most about Emily after listening to her last sentence with great interest.

'Now you're getting it. What do you like about it?' asked Emily in an encouraging voice, glad to see that Stuart was at least trying rather than just giving up.

'It's blonde,' said Stuart.

'Oh,' said Emily. Her smile dropped slightly, as she was expecting something a little more complimentary.

'I'm sorry, what I meant to say was it suits you. When I look at you do the flicking the hair back behind your ear bit, it makes my hairs stand on end,' replied Stuart as Emily looked back at him with a sort of pity in her eyes. Emily was reminded at that moment of her school days. She had been the coolest kid in the school with all her mates around her in the schoolyard at break times, and she recalled always seeing a boy in the corner who looked so cut off from everyone else. Had Stuart suffered the same fate as the unnamed kid in the corner?

'I didn't really want to ask this, but were you ever bullied or isolated when you were at school?' asked Emily in a soft voice.

Stuart didn't say anything. Instead he reached for a scrap bit of paper he had inside his jacket and wrote four capital letters on it: 'PTSD'.

'Do you know what this is?' asked Stuart, tapping it with his finger before leaning back in his chair to see Emily's response. Emily shook her head, a little frightened that Stuart had felt the need to write four letters on a piece of paper rather than give a straight answer to her basic question.

'Post-Traumatic Stress Disorder, commonly suffered by soldiers who have been in a battlefield situation,' said Stuart, not looking directly at Emily but speaking as if he were looking her in the eye.

'As a kid I was often misunderstood by everyone around me, even my own family. I had a level of intelligence with cars, bikes, and other things that was way outside of what other people called normal in the class, but having to be around other people for any length of time just caused my whole system to crash,' explained Stuart.

Crikey, have I just walked into a cryptic puzzle? thought Emily as Stuart continued his story. 'When I went to secondary school the problem only got worse. I was able to speak more, but that counted against me. I became a target to a group of people who were just completely against me and did everything they could to make my life a living hell.' Stuart tapped the bit of paper again, and this time he looked Emily straight in the eye.

'That's what school did to me. It means I struggle with relationships, I now have a lifelong hatred of education, and I'm afraid of even talking to people, let alone having friendships or a social life,' said Stuart. He trailed away, thinking back to his school days.

Emily sighed slightly, trying to take in what Stuart was telling her, but still found that he was a walking medical miracle. 'I still can't believe you went through all of that at school and still got a full-time job plus a hobby,' said Emily in amazement.

'The other stuff isn't really impressive. It's just a by-product of the Asperger's,' said Stuart.

'Oh, go on. My mother was so convinced you were an upper-class gentlemen when you came to see me the other day,' said Emily, egging him on with a slight smile.

Stuart took a deep breath before leaning back in his chair. He held out his hand in front of his face almost like he was smoking an old-fashioned pipe and said, 'Elementary, Emily, my dear,' in the same voice that he had used on Julie Green a few days earlier.

Emily started giggling, and before long she was trying with all of her strength to stop herself from roaring out loud with laughter. 'How do you do that? You must have gone to some sort of drama group or acting school,' replied Emily, wiping tears from her eyes when she regained the art of speech again.

'No, we're just born with it. Only a handful of us have this ability, though; the vast majority can't usually function like this,' said Stuart as a waiter came over to their table holding two steaming plates of food.

Stuart promptly started to separate his foods into different sections on his plates. Emily thought this a little strange, but then again, even she was known to be one for keeping things in a certain order at times. They both thanked the waiter as he strode away to top up their glasses. The rest of the evening seemed to pass quite nicely, with both Stuart and Emily in conversation about their favourite likes and general things that had come up during the day. Emily, it would seem, had been just as busy as Stuart. She had spent the last twelve months in the US state of Alabama studying American politics at the university there.

Emily had a pure love of driving and was aiming to go into politics one day. When Stuart asked what her ultimate dream car, was she showed him a picture of a silver-coloured 2012 Aston Martin DBS. Stuart being Stuart, he then spent the next five minutes or so rattling off all that he knew about Aston Martins to her, not trying to impress but to inform. Emily as usual was taken aback at how much he knew but then admitted afterwards that he would have been a great salesman for Aston Martin. Stuart grinned to himself and then wondered why he had done that. For the first time in his life he didn't feel remotely scared but instead at ease. Here was someone whom he could really relate to and not feel ashamed about talking about what he loved. Every now and again he would feel the slight pang in his stomach to tell him that danger was nearby, but he ignored it.

Stuart knew where the danger was, but he couldn't have possibly thought that Emily was going to attack him – not in the middle of having a pub meal, anyway. When they had finished eating, Stuart offered to walk with Emily back to her house a mile away or so. After ten minutes of steady walking down the country road which led into the town, Stuart suddenly stopped and looked out over the hedge down into the small valley between them and the next village to their left, which lay on top of a small hill in the distance.

'What's wrong?' said Emily, looking in the same direction as Stuart but only seeing the setting sun in the sky.

'I always forget how beautiful it is up here,' said Stuart, not looking back at her but continuing to stare at the horizon as if looking for something.

'Stu, I don't want to rush you on anything, but I do have a slight fear of the dark,' said Emily. Her voice was a little on edge now.

Stuart seemed to come to his senses as he turned back to her. 'You're right. I'm sorry; the angel must be protected,' said Stuart.

Emily looked a little surprised. 'Sorry?' she said, raising her eyebrows slightly. Stuart looked a little apprehensive at Emily's expression. After all, reading and registering other people's expressions and emotions had been a huge challenge to him since birth.

'What's the angel?' asked Emily, confused.

'Nothing,' lied Stuart, quickly thinking on the spot. He knew it was wrong not to be completely honest with her. But if he told people the truth, that he kept seeing a brown-haired woman every time he closed his eyes, then they would think he was going insane or worse.

Not saying another word, Stuart allowed Emily to carry on back to her home as he made the dark walk back towards the pub to pick up his precious Harley Davidson motorcycle. He rode back into the farmyard fifteen minutes later, making sure not to wake his family up in the process, as it was after everyone had gone to bed. He wondered why he hadn't given Emily a lift on the back of it.

As he lay on his bed that night with his eyes wide open, it suddenly occurred to Stuart that although the meal had gone quite well in terms of talking and communicating, there was still one thing that kept bugging him as he turned over and closed his eyes. Not at any point in their encounter had she attempted to give him a hug or a kiss or make any kind of sexual gesture towards him at all.

Must be early days, he thought to himself, as they had only met over dinner once. The last thought he had before he dropped off that night was, *She did look stunning, though.*

Chapter Ten

A Twenty-Year Mystery

Flashbacks were a familiar part of Stuart's life in many ways. He could be driving along a winding country road with the Road Runner on works duty somewhere in the country and then suddenly without warning, for no apparent reason, start thinking about a silly, pointless incident that meant nothing to anyone but caused Stuart a great deal of pain and suffering. His latest recollection took him back to when he was only four years old, which was his first memory of any kind of doctor's appointment. His parents sat round at a desk in the corner of the room opposite a sociologist by the name of Linda. Linda was a middle-aged woman who had spent a good part of her life in the primary school education system before going to the medical profession.

'Thanks for seeing us at such short notice. We really appreciate it,' said David. He held out his hand to shake Linda's as Abigail did the same.

'Not a problem. I was given Stuart's file when I came in this morning. You say he's been acting a little differently to the other children in his class?' said Linda in one of those soft and welcoming voices that everybody always loved and admired.

'His teachers say that he's been misbehaving, but we can't understand why,' said Abigail as Linda sat back slightly in her chair to listen.

'Misbehaving in what sort of way?' asked Linda.

'Well, there's one part of the day when all of the kids have to sit on the floor by the teacher for her morning register. When all of the kids go and sit on the carpet, Stuart doesn't go over. Instead, he separates himself from everyone else.'

When David had finished speaking, Linda looked up from her desk, having listened very closely to every word spoken. 'Usually signs of isolation aren't considered naughtiness. It might be an indication of early playground bullying,' replied Linda after a short pause.

Abigail started talking, hoping to get some other answer. 'I understand that, Linda, but it doesn't explain everything else. When Stuart's at home he always does what he's told and never misbehaves once. So why do it at school?'

David squeezed her arm as Abigail looked back at him with concern. 'I'm worried about him,' said Abigail.

David replied with a compassionate look as if to say, 'He'll be okay; it's a phase, that's all.' Linda, meanwhile, seemed to have clocked this passing of silent emotion.

'As you know we ran some tests on Stuart earlier today when you came in to us about his unusualness at school. We found that his traits are similar to that of a brain-related disorder we've been researching over the last couple of years.'

At this latest statement David and Abigail both sat up straight on a razor's edge, listening carefully. 'We believe it could be a condition called Asperger's Syndrome on what's known as the autism spectrum,' said Linda.

Both David and Abigail looked a little surprised. 'Sorry to sound a bit ignorant at this moment in time, Linda, but what's autism?' asked David. Linda pulled out a file and laid it on the desk in front of her.

'At this point in his early development we should have expected more of a social aspect to his childhood, including the ability to play and imagine with youngsters of his own age group. This, I'm afraid to say, is non-existent in Stuart at this present time,' explained Linda as she pointed out the results of the test on the sheet of paper before them on the desk.

'But what's that got to do with this autism thing?' said Abigail.

'He displays symptoms close to what is known as autism spectrum disorder, including not being able to read or understand basic body language, very specific interests in one area, and little or no interest in others,' replied Linda. For the next minute or so there was an awkward silence, which made the already quiet room sound even quieter still.

Whilst David and Abigail sat there trying to take in what was being said, Stuart happily sat in the corner with the small model of a scarlet red 1980 Audi Quattro exactly like the one featured in the BBC drama series *Ashes to Ashes.* All three of them looked round at him as he crawled around opening all of the doors as well as looking under the bonnet.

'Prop-shaft, gearbox, carburettor,' said Stuart, poking his finger underneath the bonnet.

David grinned, and Linda let out a slight chuckle. 'Mechanic in the making! He's more than welcome to come and fix my car if he wants,' said Linda in a jokey voice, looking back at David and Abigail.

'Don't give him ideas. He already tried to fix our car before he even started school,' said David as Linda grinned again.

'Is there a cure?' said Abigail so suddenly that even Linda blinked several times in surprise.

'Cure? Autism is not a disease, Mrs Robson. What Stuart has is not a disease; it's more of a gift than anything else,' said Linda as David took hold of Abigail's hand and gave it a little squeeze.

'I think what Abigail is trying to say is, will Stuart ever be able to function on his own when we're not around anymore to be there for him?' asked David in one of those voices that was trying to sound cheerful but trailed away.

Linda paused for a second. She had hoped to avoid this question, but it was coming out anyway. 'Do you mean to say, will he be able to live what you might deem a normal life?' asked Linda, wondering if this was the denial process that her colleagues had warned her about when she had first started training as a therapist.

'Yes, I do,' replied David. Abigail was curling her fingers in her lap like someone waiting for the results of a lottery draw.

'At this stage in the diagnosis it's impossible to say whether Stuart will be able to cope in later life. As far as living independently goes, this is going to prove to be a real challenge for not just him but for you as a family as well,' said Linda as she picked a file up off the desk and shoved it into one of the drawers beside her.

'Whatever you decide to do, he knows that he will be given the best help possible by parents who love and adore him and respect him for who he is,' finished Linda, leading Stuart over to them. They both took this as the cue to leave.

'I still don't know how we can do it. I mean, what can we do?' said Abigail as she filled up the kettle before placing it on the stove a few hours later back in the kitchen at the farmhouse.

'If you're thinking private education, then that's out of the question. I may run my own business, but even that wouldn't cover those sorts of costs,' said David, who was seated at the kitchen table working everything through in his mind.

'I don't know how to go about it. Even if we could afford it, would he qualify to get the help he needed?' said Abigail. David stood up and walked over to where Abigail stood over by the sink, staring out of the window at the open fields.

'I suppose he'll just have to go through mainstream,' said David but dropped away quickly.

Abigail had suddenly gone very quiet. David caught sight of a lonely tear which had run off of her face into the sink. Sensing that this whole conversation had affected Abigail in a way beyond speech, David wrapped his arms around her in a hug and gave her a small kiss on the cheek.

'Stuart's going to be okay; I bet it's just a phase he's going through. He'll grow out of it,' said David as Abigail sniffled.

'It's not that. Our son is going to go through life in a world that doesn't appreciate or understand him, and it's going to be hell for him,' said Abigail. She was trying to fight back having a full-blown breakdown in front of her husband. The kettle whistled at that moment, and David moved away to make tea, leaving Abigail still staring absentmindedly out of the window at the setting sun on the horizon.

The couple were little aware that Stuart sat on the stairs a few yards away, listening into the conversation between his parents and wondering why his mother sounded very upset. In everyone else's eyes what Stuart was doing was in effect a spying operation on his parents, but at his age he would not have known or fully understood that. Stuart himself, who had been sat there for well over ten minutes listening in, decided that he had heard enough. Not wanting to be found on the stairs by his parents, he silently slipped away up the stairs into his bedroom before burying himself under the bed covers, trying to shut out what had been said in the last few moments. The same word kept chasing itself round his brain: Why? Why was he not going to understand the world? Why would he need private education?

It was a long time until Stuart eventually managed to fall asleep after doing so much thinking that his whole brain shut itself down under the strain. 'Did you hear something?' said Abigail, suddenly turning to see the closed kitchen door leading to the main hallway.

'Probably just the timbers. This place creaks more than ever these days,' said David with a slight smile, thinking that the sudden creak outside the door was of a pair of feet moving its way up the stairs out of easy listening distance.

Coming back to the present day was always the hardest part. Twenty years later the fully grown adult Stuart was thinking back to that fateful night all those years ago when his parents sat talking about him in the kitchen. It all made sense to him now why they thought he would need private guidance.

I don't know why they bothered sending me to school. All it ever did was give me the fear of being attacked every other day, thought Stuart as he cleaned up the cylinder head gasket value on Thunderbolt's V10 turbo-driven engine. Once again he had lifted the engine out of its holdings and onto the workbench, doing his usual to label all of the components. He had the hope that by stripping down and rebuilding the modified race engine, he could not only make it run better than before but also do away with his system of labelling the many different components. Further up the bench Ben had also managed a whole cylinder block refit by himself – closely monitored by Stuart, of course. This being a home-made engine, each of the parts had come from different manufactures: Ford, BMW, Mercedes-Benz, and Audi part boxes were stacked neatly on the bench.

'Wow, this is brilliant. Nicely done, Ben. I'll make a mechanic out of you yet,' said Stuart as Ben handed him back the finished cylinder block. Stuart inspected it for any defects. For any amateur mechanic the cylinder block was by far the most important part of the engine, as it aligned the cylinders in the familiar V-shaped formation. Getting it back on the sump part of the engine was always easier said than done, as the block itself had to be aligned with the cylinders. As they both struggled with the engine block, Stuart's ears suddenly pricked up. For the smallest of seconds it sounded like a small car had rolled up outside of the shutter door.

'What's up?' said Ben, who had noticed Stuart's change in attention.

'Four-cylinder engine, sounds a little worn in quality; low revs on approach,' said Stuart. Ben guessed what he was trying to do. Stuart could tell who was coming towards him just by listening to the sound of the engines on each vehicle. It was always a fun party trick to do on unsuspecting visitors. Thinking that he had imagined it, Stuart turned back to Ben and shrugged as they both finished off fitting the cylinder block back into alignment.

'Yes!' said Ben, raising both fists in the air. With a clang like a bell, the top half of the engine was finished. Stuart kept his face blank, knowing there was still more to finish.

'Do you ever stop tinkering with that thing?' came a familiar voice from the doorway. Stuart turned to look.

Emily Green stood there leaning up against the doorway, allowing the outside light to brighten up the warehouse unit at the Robson Transport yard on the small industrial estate out of town. 'Emily,' said Stuart in a cheerful voice as she smiled slightly again. Without warning Stuart got up from his chair, strode to the door, and embraced her with a hug – which, thanks to Stuart's pure size and strength, was more like a tight squeeze. Emily winced slightly as Stuart broke away, but she restrained herself from showing any pain.

'Just routine maintenance; every time I take Thunderbolt out and race it on the track I always pull the engine straight out afterwards, clean it up, and replace any parts that have been corroded,' replied Stuart to Emily's comment as Ben pulled out the rocker arms out of a small box.

Being a little nervous in social situations, Ben would often keep himself to himself. When Stuart was around other people whom Ben didn't really know very well, he would often try to avoid their eyes or not talk to them at all if he could help it. So when Emily walked in, he just carried on working on the engine.

'Why do you have to do that? Isn't just taking it apart once complicated enough?' said Emily in a light, jokey voice as Stuart led her over to the open bonnet area in the front of Thunderbolt. For the next ten minutes or so Stuart stood by Emily's side launching into his speech with the technical information about how rebuilding the engine helped keep speed up and lap times down.

'Who's your friend? I've never seen him before,' said Emily once her brain had yet again been pushed to a breaking point through the amount of information given to her by Stuart and his mechanical expertise.

'Oh, that's my friend Ben; I've known him since my first year in secondary school. He's a bit of a shy person, really, so he tends to keep himself to himself most of the time,' said Stuart. He watched Ben busying himself by taking one of the piston heads over to the sink in the corner and washing in paraffin to clean out all of the muck and junk that had built up during its running time.

'Aww, bless him,' said Emily, grinning slightly and doing her usual of brushing her hair back behind her ear.

'You're just in time. I was running some tests with the on-board features I've got with Thunderbolt,' said Stuart, opening the driver's side door before climbing inside.

Emily stuck her head inside of the cockpit and was taken aback by the amount of equipment on board along with the specialised racing seats and long-range fuel tank along the back seats as well as in the boot along with the black metal roll cage. 'Wow, it's like a spaceship in here,' said Emily. On the dashboard was just a single computer screen no bigger than a tablet iPad.

'This is what I'm especially proud of; this is the technical readout, which is linked in via an Internet connection giving me the same information the pit crews have during a race,' said Stuart as he turned it on and flicked through the settings. These included brake usage readouts and a G-meter for cornering forces along with other useful features.

'That's incredible,' said Emily, looking in awe at the sort of skills that were being used on the autistic level by Stuart. At this point there was a small tap just in front of him. Stuart and Emily looked up to see Ben standing in front of the car waving at them.

'Engine's done; it's ready to go back in now,' said Ben. He walked back across the room to the crane, which was ready to lower the engine back into the engine bay.

'Thanks for that, Ben,' said Stuart. Emily quickly moved out of the way to allow Stuart to jump out of the car and help Ben roll the newly rebuilt engine on its crane to the front of the car to refit it in.

'Can I help?' asked Emily as she saw the engine swinging slightly on its slings on the mobile crane. Ben was hanging on the driving end, trying to steady it.

'Sure. This is usually a one-person operation, but as long as we don't drop the engine through the car we should be okay,' said Stuart with a slight laugh. Emily also gave a little laugh and stared down into the engine bay to line up the mounting bolts with the holes in the engine where the two connected.

'On my command, lower in,' said Stuart, moving round to the right-hand side of the engine and pushing down on the rear of the engine.

'Now,' he said as Ben pushed down on the crane.

'Okay,' said Emily, quickly giving a thumbs-up. With a slight banging sound, the engine landed smoothly on its mounting bolts. The moment the engine was down inside the engine bay, Stuart slid underneath the car. Ben handed him some bolts which connected the exhaust system and other pipes under the car.

'Can you finish off, Ben? I need to get some fuel in the tank to test fire the engine,' said Stuart, sliding out from underneath. He and Ben swapped places. Emily at this point seemed too scared to even move an inch in case she tripped one of them up or knocked over something important. She instead decided to focus on Stuart, who was dragging a pipe connected to an oil drum with the word 'Gas' written on the side; clearly it was made by an American company. Stuart pushed the end of the pipe into the fuel filler and turned the tap on. A second or so later there was a spurt of fuel as the tap was shut off, and he pulled the pipe away to allow for the test fire to begin.

'Ready, Ben?' asked Stuart, jumping back into the car and inserting a red safety key into the ignition.

'Ready,' said Ben, sliding himself out from underneath Thunderbolt and moving over towards the wall.

'Hang on, Emily,' said Stuart. Emily, now not as scared as before, moved towards Stuart.

'Would you like to do the honours?' asked Stuart, gesturing to the red safety key in the ignition slot.

'Yes, okay,' said Emily excitedly. Secretly she'd wanted to do this sort of thing all along for years. Emily placed her hand on the switch as Stuart and Ben covered their ears. Emily wondered why they had done that; surely the engine wasn't that loud. She soon found out it wasn't. A second later the engine roared into life with such force the car rocked slightly on its springs.

'Wow!' shouted Emily over the noise as she revved the throttle a few times, enjoying the sound that the V10 engine made even just on the tick-over.

Suddenly and without warning the air was filled with clouds of white smoke. Stuart swore loudly, but before he could get anywhere near the ignition key the whole engine cut out. All three of them started coughing loudly as smoke filled the warehouse unit, making it look like the whole building was on fire. As the shutter door was up, the smoke disappeared quite quickly.

Stuart stood there with his hands on his hips breathing slowly, not wanting to inhale the fumes. 'Well, that's an interesting feature,' said Emily as Stuart banged his head on the car's bodywork.

'What's the technical term for white smoke coming out of the exhausts again?' said Ben. Stuart picked himself up again, looking straight at Ben this time.

Emily was a little frightened, thinking she'd done something wrong. *Oh damn, have I just broken Stuart's pride and joy?* thought Emily, wondering what to do or say next.

Stuart looked a little tired and frustrated. 'Ben, can you fetch the crane? We're going to need to take that engine out again,' said Stuart as Ben nodded in agreement.

'Stuart, I really didn't mean to break your car,' said Emily, sounding quite emotional now.

But Stuart seemed to display a level of compassion at this point. 'It's not your fault, Emily. I didn't look at what sort of fuel I was putting in the tank,' said Stuart as he pointed towards the oil drum. Emily looked confused, but then it suddenly twigged what Stuart was on about.

'This is a diesel car, isn't it?' said Emily. Stuart nodded slowly.

'I shouldn't have turned the key. It's going to take months to rebuild that engine,' said Emily.

Stuart shook his head in disagreement. 'No, not at all. I should have a full rebuild done in one day. That's not a problem.' He waved his hand in front of him, sounding like it was no problem at all. Emily seemed a little relieved and surprised that Stuart was taking the situation calmly and without fuss.

'I hope you don't mind me asking, but are all of you like this?' asked Emily.

'What do you mean?' said Stuart, smiling slightly.

'I mean to say, are you all this calm and relaxed?' said Emily.

Stuart felt his brain go a little funny. 'Most of us are, when we have the right training and support. Why yell and shout at people? That doesn't fix or mend anything. It just makes things worse,' replied Stuart.

Chapter Eleven

The Expected and the Unexpected

Over the next couple of days Stuart and Ben rebuilt the V10 engine after its episode with the misfiring cylinders. Emily had gone a little quiet towards Stuart after the accident, but she had said afterwards that she wanted to pay him back for breaking Thunderbolt, even though he told her quite plainly it wasn't her fault. Feeling a little guilty for the whole situation himself, Stuart had given her a ticket to his next track day, but he also had another trick up his sleeve. After consulting with Ben he had decided that the best way to make it up to Emily would be to surprise her with a gift if the opportunity ever came along.

And so it was that Stuart and Ben, along with a very confused twin brother Adam, found themselves outside Emily Green's house in the dark with a twelve-ton breakdown recovery truck borrowed from Robson Transport. Stuart reversed the lorry up the driveway towards the group of cars parked up in a fan shape.

'This is wrong; this is so wrong,' said Ben, who couldn't believe what he was doing.

'You can't just take someone's car away from their house and expect them to be all right about it,' said Adam as Stuart opened his door and jumped down.

'We're not stealing it; we're borrowing it. Now come on quick; Emily's going to be home any minute now,' said Stuart. The two of them ran round to the back whilst Adam kept his eyes on the road ahead, looking for an unsuspecting Emily.

Using a remote control and a highly powerful winch mounted on the back of the cab, they managed to pull Emily's black Ford Fiesta up the ramp onto the back of the truck without problems. At that moment a light appeared at one of the windows as Rick Green appeared at the window pulling back the curtain to see what was going on. Stuart caught sight of him and gave him the thumbs-up. Rick returned it and closed the curtains again as Stuart and Ben returned to the cab. As it turned out, they were not a moment too soon; the rear door flung open as Adam hopped in, telling them Emily was coming down the road on foot. Stuart pulled out of the driveway, making his way back towards his home. The following morning Emily stepped out of her front door holding her car keys, ready to head out to meet some friends across town.

When she pushed the button on the key to open her car and didn't hear a return beeping, her first thought was that it must have broken again, even though it had only been at the garage a few days earlier. As she looked up from her phone, Emily's eyes widened in shock to see an empty space where her car should have been.

'Oh my god,' exclaimed Emily as Rick stuck his head out of the upstairs window.

'Heard you shout, Emily. What's up?' said Rick.

'Dad, where's my car?' said Emily, trying her best at this point not to panic.

'Sorry, Emily. It was meant to be a surprise for you later,' said Rick with a slight smile on his face.

'What surprise? Where's my car gone?' replied Emily, pocketing her keys as she knew now that she wouldn't need them.

'Stuart came last night and picked it up; he's going to do some work on it for you,' said Rick.

Emily looked stunned. 'Stuart's got my car?' she replied.

'Don't worry, nothing bad is going to happen to it. He's got it at his house, but it's a bit of a way out of town,' said Rick as Emily sprinted away down the driveway towards the end of the road. Being quite physically fit and healthy, she was able to reach the outskirts of the town very quickly and soon found herself at the turning on the main road running down to the Robson farmhouse. Jogging down the lane, she soon found herself in the farmyard. She noticed the sheeted Thunderbolt through the open barn door. Emily walked towards it, but before she could reach it a voice came across the yard.

'Hi, Emily. I wasn't expecting you till later today,' said Stuart, climbing down from the Fordson Major Tractor which had just come in off the open grass field behind the farmhouse.

'My dad told me what you'd done with my car. It wasn't much that needed doing; I only needed a new exhaust silencer box,' said Emily, a little out of breath.

Stuart came over to her, splashing a little in the mud covering the yard as his wellies squelched underfoot. 'I did work that one out. When I fired it up it sounded like someone had fitted an after-market exhaust to it,' said Stuart as they both moved across the yard towards the barn. With a wide grin on his face, Stuart grabbed hold of the brown sheet and gave it a huge tug. It fell to the floor, revealing the newly improved midnight black Ford Fiesta. But he hadn't just fixed the silencer box on the underside.

Emily clapped a hand to her mouth in shock at what she was seeing, almost the same as someone who had been secretly filmed on a hidden camera TV program. The Fiesta had a gleam about it that she hadn't seen before; the headlights were shining brightly, being free of dirt and muck behind the glass lens. All of the door handles had been resprayed, and the alloy wheels had been re-buffed so they were as good as new ones.

'How?' said Emily in pure amazement, having finally pulled her hands away from her mouth.

'There wasn't really much to do. The whole car itself is in a pretty good condition, so it didn't take me as long as I thought,' said Stuart, who was starting to feel the pangs in his mind again. *Tell her now, go on; everything will be fine*, came the smooth, understanding voice in his head again.

Stuart wasn't at all shocked by this voice but still took a deep breath and steeled himself to the question that he felt was going to be the most important of his life to date.

'Are you all right?' asked Emily as Stuart went a little white.

'Emily, you know I always thought that we could be really good friends,' said Stuart as Emily smiled.

'Only good friends would steal my car in the dark and take it away to give it a full restoration,' said Emily in a jokey voice as Stuart relaxed a little.

He pulled out a small red box and knelt down on one knee. At the sight of this sudden move, Emily gasped in shock and backed into the wall. She widened her eyes in shock, not feeling happy and warm but having a sense of wanting to run away as fast as possible, the same as Stuart had felt whilst the two of them sat having a meal together.

'I know how this looks, but I've wanted to ask this for a long time. And I feel that if I don't have the courage now, then I never will,' said

Stuart, opening the small box in front of him to show a gleaming golden engagement ring nestled inside.

'Emily, will you be my girlfriend, to be my undivided love and care in all my heart?' said Stuart, the words getting stuck in his throat.

Emily, still in shock from all this, relaxed a little as she realised that he wasn't proposing to her but asking her for a relationship. 'Oh Stu, I am sorry; I am truly sorry,' said Emily, shaking her head a little. Stuart, completely unaware of what was going on in her mind, continued to kneel on the barn floor holding out the ring to her.

'I won't admit that I'm not in shock about this; I never knew that you felt this way about me,' replied Emily.

Then the penny dropped with a horrible clang, although it wasn't a penny that dropped but the golden ring, which fell from Stuart's hand and hit the floor, echoing all around the barn.

'I'm already seeing someone else. I've got a boyfriend,' said Emily slowly in a calm, collected voice. But by then it was too late. Stuart knelt there frozen in shock as Emily stepped into her car and rolled the window down to look at him.

'I have to go. Thanks again for the car; I'm so sorry,' replied Emily as she started the engine and drove slowly away up the lane towards the main road.

It was a few minutes after the black Ford Fiesta had disappeared from view before Stuart, still kneeling on the floor, let out a small wince. 'Why me?' said Stuart, his voice cracking. He fell to the floor unable to speak, now feeling his eyes start to flood with tears.

Although Stuart never showed his feelings as much as others, emotions ran so deep within people with autism and Asperger's that the news of what most people would recognise as a rejection hit Stuart with the same force as a speeding train would.

So much for the whole 'stiff upper lip' thing. You and Mum never had this problem, thought Stuart, recalling what David had once told him about overcoming the uncontrollable wave of emotions crashing in around him. Meanwhile, a few miles down the road, Emily had been shaken up as much as Stuart had by the incident in the barn. She had driven straight back home to find a completely empty house, as the rest of her family were all out at their workplaces.

Once she had parked the Fiesta, Emily raced into the kitchen, grabbing a cup off the side before making for the sink. She filled the cup with tap water and downed the whole lot in one go. Breathing heavily, she ran her hands through her hair, trying to be calm about the whole situation. But there was no other way around it. Going on the so-called dinner date with Stuart in the first place seemed to have given him the impression that maybe she liked him. He had taken this on and somehow seen her as a lover-boy rescue worker rather than a relationship mentor.

Emily jumped slightly as the front door swung open. Julie Green stepped inside with two carrier bags, having just been to the local shops.

'Hi, Emily. What are you doing here? I thought you were seeing your friends in the town today,' said Julie, walking through to the kitchen and placing the bags down on the worktop. Her expression suddenly changed to concern, however, when she saw the look on Emily's face.

'Darling, what's the matter? You haven't been dumped by your boyfriend, have you?' said Julie in a calming, concerned voice, placing her arm around Emily as she hung her head.

'What have I done?' said Emily as she tried very hard to fight back the tears now welling in her eyes. Julie at this point started rubbing her hand up and down Emily's back, trying to comfort her, but it didn't seem to be doing any good.

'What was he even thinking of?' continued Emily. Julie stopped comforting her and sat down in the kitchen chair.

Without waiting to be asked for an explanation, Emily launched into her story of what had happened to her with Stuart. She covered everything from the first time they met in the warehouse unit at the Robson Transport depot to the events that had happened less than half an hour earlier in the Robson house farmyard. When she had finished talking, Emily poured herself another mug of water before sitting back down at the kitchen table again.

'Aww, that's so sweet of him to go out of his way to do that,' said Julie when she had heard the story of Stuart making the gold ring himself before getting down on one knee and asking her to be his girlfriend.

'That's not the point, though. What am I going to do now?' said Emily as Julie sighed and placed her hands together, having a think.

'I don't know what to do. Should I go back to Stuart or just ignore him?' said Emily, turning to Julie for an answer.

'You already know the answer to that. Just look into your heart, and it will tell you the solution,' said Julie in one of those voices that reminded people of the way that nuns and vicars always spoke during a confession period.

Emily hung her head again and nodded, knowing what the outcome was going to be. She had come to the decision that she couldn't see Stuart anymore after his way of approaching her about an actual relationship.

'I hope nothing bad happens after this,' said Emily, but she knew that this possibility was just a wild fantasy at best. Back at the Robson farmhouse, things couldn't have been more fragile even if they were wrapped up in a sealed box reading 'this way up' in big black letters.

Chapter Twelve

The Angel and the Departed

Stuart spent days in the barn, trying all he could to take his mind off of the fact that the woman he loved above all others had just admitted her love to someone else. Past memories, bad experiences, and the same last words spoken by Emily Green to him now echoed in his ears as he pulled apart the cylinder block, wiping the bit of rag all around the inner casing and smearing it with oil. The same word kept repeating itself over and over again in his head: Boyfriend, boyfriend, boyfriend. Feeling the whole world had been against him from the very beginning of his life, Stuart let out a cry like a wounded animal before picking up a spanner off the bench and launching it into the air so hard that it embedded itself in the wall opposite him with a loud bang.

He had to admit his aim was still pretty good despite being so apocalyptically angry at the whole situation. How could she do something like that to him? *Hadn't I been kind enough to her?* he thought. Then something in the back of his mind seemed to be telling him what to do. *Go for a ride; that's always what you do when you're frustrated*, said the voice in his head. Stuart didn't need telling twice. As if following orders he headed straight for the corner of the barn, where his favourite Harley Davidson motorcycle sat under its usual sheet. Grabbing hold of the sheet, he gave it a sharp tug to let the dust blow off the blanket as it fell to the floor before mounting the bike and kicking it into life. Its engine roared as Stuart pulled his crash helmet on over his head and headed straight out into the darkening countryside around him.

Out on the open road, he opened the throttle and felt the full acceleration of the Harley Davidson as it picked up speed: twenty, forty, sixty. It seemed the impulse for speed had returned. As the needle passed sixty-five, he felt the glare of a large vehicle's headlights moving towards him at speed. The next thing he knew there was a long blast of a truck's air horn. Stuart swerved sideways, avoiding it by inches, only to find another beam of lights directly ahead. A ringing silence followed. It felt like it was all over in a trice. The last thing he remembered was a loud crash as he was thrown head first into the windscreen of the people carrier on the opposite side of the road. He skidded over the top before coming to rest flat on his back on the road behind the car that had hit him.

The next thing he remembered he was on his back, staring up not at the darkening Hertfordshire country sky but instead at a very bright room which seemed to have nothing in it except funny-shaped silhouettes. Gingerly he sat up, slowly taking in the faint shapes around him. One by one they started to come into focus. The first was the Harley Davidson motorcycle he'd been riding, which looked quite undamaged considering it had just had a head-on collision with a car three times its size and weight. Along from the Harley came the faithful Thunderbolt race car complete with its stickers and racing bodywork. They seemed to be floating past him all on their own, as Stuart wasn't moving. He just stood there watching them pass him until suddenly his senses picked up.

There had been sound just feet away from him, as if a set of high-heeled shoes had been there just a fraction of a second earlier. 'It's said that when people are in their final moments they see their loved ones flash before their eyes. But that doesn't seem to be the case with you, does it?' said a sudden, light voice from right behind him. Stuart jumped so much he felt like someone had come running at him brandishing a knife. He spun round on the spot in a standard attack position but stopped short when he saw who had spoken a second ago. It seemed he was not alone in this current dreamlike state. Out of the fading mist all around him came a slim, brown-haired woman dressed in what looked like an official skirt and blouse not unlike the sort of thing worn by a secretary in the office of a company's chief executive.

She walked forward slowly and sat herself down on a park bench which had come along with the car and the bike. In a surreal way, she was right. Why, if these were his last moments after the crash, were the two things he thought of the Thunderbolt race car and the Harley motorcycle, not his family or friends? Was he somehow careless? Or maybe his Asperger's made him focused on vehicles and not people. It won't have been the first time. Emily's face swam in front of him. Her face soon vanished, however, as his attention was brought back to where he was.

'I don't understand. Who are you? One second I was on the bike, and then I'm here,' said Stuart in confusion, looking all around him before fixing his gaze back on the woman now seated on the bench.

'Why don't you sit down? I'm sure you have a lot to ask,' said the woman, patting her hand beside her on the bench. Stuart did as he was instructed and sat down, looking nervous, before turning to face the woman, who was now fixing him with a smile that told him that she had a bit of a soft spot for him.

'I blame myself, you know. I started this,' said the woman.

'Blame you? What for?' asked Stuart in confusion.

'I never introduced myself. My name is Sophie; it stands for Sub Operating Physiology Highly Intelligent Engineering.'

'It's you! You're the one I keep seeing when I'm asleep,' exclaimed Stuart. Sudden realisation crashed in around him.

'That's right, you've got me,' said Sophie, holding her hands up in a mock gesture of surrender followed by a broad grin.

She suddenly reacted so fast that Stuart sat bolt upright, afraid that his own sub consciousness was going to attack him. 'Don't be afraid, Stu. I'm not going to hurt you, just do a spot of light reading,' explained Sophie. She reached into what looked like her handbag and pulled out a pair of glasses and a red book, which she quickly opened and flicked through, studying it carefully.

'Ah, here we are, your last chapter. A motorcycle accident! That's never anything good to end on,' said Sophie out loud with her nose still in the red book.

Stuart attempted to peer in to look, but Sophie pulled it sharply out of his gaze. 'Sorry about this, but you shouldn't know about your own future,' said Sophie.

'That book has my future in it?' said Stuart in surprise.

'Damn, I knew I shouldn't have installed that spoiler alert software,' muttered Sophie to herself as she flicked through the pages.

'But this is brilliant. I knew it! People thought I was crazy when I talked about this voice in my head advising me about girls and life, yet here I am talking to you right now. But I can see you in a human form,' said Stuart excitedly. Sudden blisters of truth popped in front of his eyes like balloons.

Sophie grinned at this point, showing her brilliantly white teeth, before reading on. 'According to your system checks carried out over the years, it seems that relationships were a troubling problem for you, Oh this is interesting – Emily.'

Stuart's eyes narrowed for a second, and it seemed like he was trying to fight back the urge to throw a punch at the wall.

'Please don't say that name; it's almost like she haunts me, like a nightmare,' said Stuart as Sophie placed her hand on his knee.

'Finding out there's a boyfriend on the scene can never be easy,' replied Sophie.

'Why did she do that? She must have known even from the first time I met her. How can you have a boyfriend and not notice? He must have been in contact with her twenty-four seven,' exclaimed Stuart, standing up and starting to pace up and down.

Sophie took off her glasses and closed the book before placing it down on the bench next to her. For the smallest of seconds Stuart was tempted to make a grab for it but then decided against it. His reflexes may have been very quick, but she was seated right next to it and would have got there first.

'Can I give you a bit of advice?' said Sophie, not in a patronising way but in a very soft voice.

Stuart stopped pacing to look at Sophie as she made a gesture for him to sit back down with her. Stuart sat back down as Sophie turned to look at him. 'Do you often find it hard to express your feelings to someone else?' she asked, still in her calm voice.

Stuart nodded, unable to speak at this point. It seemed all of his systems had started to shut down. He tried to start up his mind box to create a shield around himself to stop his emotions getting the better of him but found it blank. Then he was hit with a sudden thought: maybe this was his mind box. Somehow he had become a prisoner inside it, surrounded by all of his emotions and feelings with no means of escape. But that couldn't have been right. Once upon a time he had a name for this sort of situation: dark territory.

'Speaking from a female perspective, it can be quite difficult to get our feelings across to the boys sometimes, as we can't always understand them,' said Sophie.

Stuart gave a small chuckle of laughter. 'Tell me about it. You know, when I was at school I used to think that all girls came from another planet somewhere out in the far reaches of the universe. All that stuff about making themselves look nice and the whole fashion thing – I never completely understood it,' exclaimed Stuart. Frustration came to the surface again, as it always did in these sort of situations.

Sophie smiled again and let out a little giggle of laughter. 'What's so funny?' asked Stuart, a little taken aback at Sophie's laugh.

'Ah, Stu, you are funny sometimes. Emily was lucky to meet you,' said Sophie. But she quickly stopped, as Stuart's expression of confusion had turned to one of annoyance.

'Don't listen to what your head's telling you, Stu. Listen to your heart,' said Sophie.

'What's the difference? She doesn't love me. She made that clear to me when she told me about her so-called boyfriend, whom she failed to mention until after all of these times of seeing one another,' replied Stuart, looking ready to start pacing again.

Sophie was on her feet this time, Stuart seemed to stand up instinctively, even though his brain hadn't told him to do it. 'Remember this: Your head will never forget, but your heart will always forgive,' said Sophie as she reached out to hold his hands.

'Aggh,' he said, suddenly recoiling slightly as what felt like an electric charge passed through his body. 'What in the world was that?'

Sophie didn't say anything. Her fingers came in again, but this time his fighter pilot reflexes kicked in. He managed to grab hold of her hands before they could make contact with his skin again. Sophie gave a sharp cry of pain, but as soon as Stuart had released her arms from his grip, she prodded him in the chest again. The shock that came through this time was so strong that Stuart was blasted backwards onto the floor, landing on his back on what felt like solid tarmac. He felt pains in his back as well as in his chest.

Sophie knelt down next to him, letting her hair drop down to the floor. As she did her face lit up with a smile that made his senses skyrocket. He saw her true beauty in his eyes, which had slightly dilated.

'Clear,' she said suddenly, not in her usual soft voice but in a man's voice much deeper than her own.

Stuart stared for a second. Before he could fathom what was happening, he felt the electric shock again, and this time it brought him back to his senses. There were the sounds of sirens, running diesel engines, and hurried footsteps along with blue and white flashing lights all around him. His nostrils were suddenly filled with the strong smell of petrol. The fuel tank on his bike must have ruptured on impact. He was aware of a man wearing a high-visibility jacket leaning over him.

'I've got a pulse,' said a voice. Stuart felt a pair of fingers pushed into the side of his neck, feeling his pulse getting stronger by the minute. The word 'Paramedic' flashed across his vision as Stuart took in the man now leaning over him.

'Stuart, can you hear me?' came the paramedic's voice. Stuart felt his eyelid being forced open, and he was blinded by a bright light in his eyeballs. He felt his whole body start to fill with life again. He suddenly sat bolt upright on the ground, sending the paramedic flying backwards with his hidden power and agility. Immediately after this

Stuart felt himself being swamped with people who were trying to hold him still on the ground. The paramedic injected an anaesthetic into him, thinking he was having an epileptic fit.

'Don't do that,' said Stuart as loudly as he could, but the people around him didn't seem to hear him. One of the paramedics approached with a needle containing morphine. At the sight of this Stuart managed to break free of the two paramedics and a police officer who were attempting to keep him still.

He was up on his feet and away but then a second later promptly slammed into the side of the box ambulance parked less than ten yards away. 'Oh crud,' said Stuart like the cartoon character Elma Thud usually did before falling backwards onto the floor out cold. The last thing he remembered before he blacked out was the sight of blue flashing lights and the eyes of the paramedics staring down at him, shocked at what had just happened.

Chapter Thirteen

Hospital Aftermath

'I don't know what he was thinking. He shouldn't have been out on that bike, not after what he'd just been through,' came Abigail's voice from what felt like a long way away.

'Stuart's strong. But I admit what happened was really bad,' said David in a worried voice.

'Bad? David, have you gone out of your mind? We nearly just lost our son back there. I tell you, when I find the driver who caused his crash I'll skin them alive,' exclaimed Abigail, trying to keep her voice under control.

There seemed to be a pause for a second before Stuart heard the voices of his parents start off again. 'Well, at least we know he wasn't speeding. The police told me that the Harley's speedometer froze at fifty-eight at the moment of impact. In a court of law that's hard evidence to prove that Stuart was not at fault,' said David as there was a creak of chairs.

Stuart felt warmth wrapped around him. Although had regained full consciousness, he still kept his eyes clamped shut, listening to the conversation that was happening in the room with him. There was a click as Stuart heard the sound of the door opening and footsteps coming in. Whoever it was wore heavy shoes or even boots.

'Mr and Mrs Robson,' said a calm voice that Stuart didn't recognise. By the way this man spoke Stuart could tell that he was in a public service role. That's what his Asperger's was telling him, anyway. 'I'm P. C. Ryan Philips. I was the first on the scene after the collision.'

'Is Stuart okay?' asked Abigail, grasping David's arm and bracing herself for the news that no parent ever wanted to hear.

'Stuart's going to be okay. The doctors have looked him over, and from what they were telling me there's no lifelong lasting injuries,' said P. C. Philips.

'You sound surprised,' said David, as P. C. Philips' voice had sounded a little different towards the end of his last statement.

'When the paramedics arrived and did a physical check on Stuart, they told me that a motorcycle impact at that speed could have been fatal and would have caused broken bones at the very least. Yet all they could find was just light bruising, as if he had just slid along the ground rather than suffering a head-on impact,' explained P. C. Philips, trying to keep his voice steady but feeling at a loss himself.

'I always knew he was a tough nut,' said David.

Abigail was close to tears at the sight of her eldest son lying on the hospital bed. 'He's on the autistic spectrum. The condition's called Asperger's Syndrome. He's lived with it all his life,' said Abigail, unable to contain herself anymore.

'Sorry to sound a little ignorant, but what does that mean exactly?' said P. C. Philips in a confused voice but with an air of a detective investigating a suspect at a crime scene.

'It makes us able to see life, the universe, and everything else in a way that other people could only dream of,' said Stuart out loud, not moving and still with his eyes closed.

David swore and jumped backwards, nearly tripping over his chair in the process. Abigail let out a small scream in surprise at Stuart's sudden sentence, and P. C. Philips jumped so much his hand went for his pocket, where he usually kept his Taser stun-gun.

'God in heaven, Stu, will you not do that?' said David, clutching his chest as if he had just had a heart attack.

'Sorry about that. I was in mind box mode, so I would have given you all the impression I was asleep,' said Stuart, opening his eyes fully and sitting up in the bed.

'Constable Philips! A pleasure to meet you, sir,' said Stuart, extending his hand with a slight wince as a short, sharp shock of pain flew up his arm.

'And you, Mr Robson. I hope you're feeling better,' said P.C. Philips, who was feeling for his notebook, ready to take notes.

'May I?' said Stuart, reaching out for his notebook.

'Oh, err, okay,' said P. C. Philips. He handed over his notebook and a pencil to Stuart, who laid them in front of him on the bed. In the next few minutes Stuart drew out a picture in the notebook, labelling all of the neatly drawn boxes on the page. These represented the vehicles involved and where they had been at the moment of the impact. On the following page he gave a detailed account of what had happened. All this time he was doing this, his parents and P. C. Philips looked on, watching him with such interest it was almost as if he were an extra-terrestrial being. When he had finished he laid the book in front of him, placing the pencil flat against the book like someone with OCD.

'Is this what happened, Stuart?' said Abigail, taking his hand and giving it a little squeeze.

'Those are the full details, right up to the moment of impact,' said Stuart as P. C. Philips gently picked up the notebook and slowly flicked through the pages, taking in the information Stuart had left him.

'Thank you, Mr Robson. This is very helpful; I'm sure this will be strong evidence if a court case comes around,' said P. C. Philips. Stuart nodded in understanding.

David tapped P. C. Philips on the shoulder, and they both headed out of the room, closing the door behind them. 'I think it's best if you know this now rather than find it out later,' said David as P. C. Philips placed his hands inside his stab jacket and listened carefully.

'We did investigations at the scene and found that the lorry driver who pulled out of the junction was at fault for the collision; Stuart was only acting defensively, which anyone would have done in that situation,' said P. C. Philips.

'That's good news about Stuart. I don't know what we'd all do if he wasn't able to drive. He practically worships and lives on it,' said David with a small laugh.

'I've heard about autism on the radio and in the news, but I've never met anyone like Stuart. It's like he's a youngster on the surface but his mind is ahead of his time,' explained P. C. Philips.

David shrugged. 'That's just Stuart. We may never know what's really going on in his mind. He can strip down and rebuild vehicles of any size completely unaided, and yet if you ask him to cook a meal or iron clothing, for example, he just shuts down and doesn't know what to do.' They watched Abigail and Stuart talking through the glass window.

'I'd best get back to the station. I need to type some of this up,' said P. C. Philips.

'Yes, of course, thank you. I can't thank you enough,' said David as they shook hands.

'Have a nice day, Mr Robson. We'll be in touch,' said P. C. Philips. As he strode away, David went back into the room to find Stuart in a fierce discussion with Abigail.

'I don't want you on a motorbike anymore; this is proof of what I've been telling you for years,' said Abigail, not shouting as such but in a stern voice.

'I'm not giving up my bike. Ben's had two collisions in his time of biking, and he hasn't been hurt. Anyway, what am I supposed to tell him? Oh, sorry, Ben, but I can't do any more road trips with you because my mother, who knows bugger-all about driving, seems to think that by not letting me on a bike she's going to stop me getting hurt,' said Stuart, trying to keep his voice under control.

'What's going on?' said David as Abigail turned to him, hoping now that she was going to get an ally in her fight against motorcycles.

'My own mother doesn't want me on a bike anymore,' said Stuart in a sarcastic voice.

David sighed heavily, rubbing his eyes together. 'Considering the situation that's just happened, Stu, I think that your mother has a very valid point,' said David, but it seemed he had hit a nerve.

'Oh great. First I get stabbed in the back by someone I thought had a crush on me. Then I'm involved in a road traffic collision which I didn't cause, as a result of which I have a parent who's never had a problem with me riding bikes before who now hates me for doing it. Everything's always my fault, isn't it?' yelled Stuart, feeling his emotions bubbling over the top at all of his unwanted bad luck.

'I wish I had been killed back there. It would have been no big loss,' exclaimed Stuart. David and Abigail felt shocked and horrified that their son had just said that. A buzzer went off on the wall signalling the end of the visiting time.

'He didn't mean to say that. He's not in his right mind at the minute. You know in a couple of days he'll be back to the way he usually is, rebuilding his BMW and boring us all to death about cars,' said David a few hours later as the three of them sat around the dinner table after finishing off a well-cooked meal. They were constantly aware of Stuart's empty chair as they tried to talk through the things that had been happening and where to go next in terms of dealing with everything both physically and mentally.

Back at the hospital Stuart turned over onto his side, trying to bury his face into the bedclothes and wishing that the sounds outside would go away. 'Don't give up, Stu. You may want to leave this world, but this world hasn't seen the last of you yet,' said Sophie.

Stuart sat bolt upright on the bed staring at her ghostly figure sitting in one of the chairs that his parents had occupied only hours earlier. 'I don't know what to do anymore, Sophie. It seems that it doesn't matter how much I try; girls just don't give me the love and respect that I give them.'

Stuart felt the silence crash around him as he sensed Sophie nearby thinking hard about what Stuart had said. She had closed her eyes and leaned back in the chair to focus on the problem in question.

Stuart, thinking that she had gone, fell quickly asleep. But Sophie hadn't gone away. She stayed for a little while longer, watching him sleeping in the bed and thinking back to his early days, when she had first been created as part of the aid in his mind. After all, she was effectively the autistic gene; everything that happened inside Stuart's mind was thanks to her. Sophie was protected in the form of a safety mechanism. She could stop Stuart socially by making him go crazy and push people away if she wanted. But at the same time, Stuart could still stop her by way of a near-fatal injury. This would make all of his body's senses rush to action stations in order to fix the problem, not leaving enough power to run Sophie as a program. Each therefore could not live without the other.

Without Stuart, Sophie couldn't get a picture of the outside world or help him with his social problem. Without Sophie on board, Stuart was completely at a loss as to how the whole cycle of life thing worked. They were crucial to each other's survival and ability to understand the world that they had both been brought into. Sophie looked down at her hands and saw they were fading slightly. Realising she was about to dematerialise, she stood up and walked slowly towards Stuart asleep on the bed. She vanished before she reached the wall, almost like a ghost. When Stuart awoke it was to the sound of the ward nurse taking his pulse and pushing in a tray with a full English breakfast on a plate.

'Well, I might say, Mr Robson, considering the fact that you should have broken three ribs in that motorcycle crash, your body seems to be stronger than the doctors predicted,' explained the nurse.

Chapter Fourteen

A Surprising Thought

As she spoke, the nurse propped up his pillow and took his pulse following the small pocket watch attached to her uniform.

'Morning, Mr Robson. Is the nurse taking care of you?' asked the doctor, who had just pushed open the door wearing the standard-issue white lab coat and holding his usual clipboard with patient notes. Stuart nodded, as his mouth was a little full at the time. The doctor grinned as the nurse exited the room after taking some notes with her to file them outside in the corridor. All of a sudden the doctor made to seat himself down next to Stuart's bed.

'Sorry, Doctor. I won't be a second,' said Stuart.

But the doctor waved his hand in the air. 'Oh, please don't stop on my part. I only came to see how you were this morning,' said the doctor, turning back to his notes.

'Can I go soon, doc? It's only I'm supposed to be in a touring car championship at the weekend, and I don't feel any different than what I was before,' said Stuart.

The doctor looked up from his notes. 'Oh, I'm sure something can be arranged. It seems incredible that you've recovered this quickly considering the level of injury you should have sustained,' said the doctor, placing his notes down on the bedside table before turning to Stuart and starting to speak. 'I'm Doctor –'

'Graham R Trent, study of mental illness and learning difficulties,' finished Stuart as Doctor Trent suddenly looked amazed.

'Incredible! Your condition really is outstanding. You knew my name before I'd even said it,' said Doctor Trent, in awe of Stuart's abilities.

'No, I read it on your name tag,' said Stuart as Doctor Trent looked down at his chest and laughed.

'How silly of me. I should have thought to take it off before I come in,' said Doctor Trent as he looked at Stuart directly. Stuart hadn't sounded rude when he had said this last statement but had resembled a computer rolling off information that may have not been important but was still somehow worthwhile.

'I was really hoping to meet you before you were discharged. In fact, you seem to be one of our unusual cases in here,' said Doctor Trent as he looked into Stuart's face.

'Okay. So what did you want to know?' said Stuart, not in a patronising voice but in a calm one. He attempted to sit up straight, pushing his pillows up behind him as Doctor Trent straightened the papers on his clipboard. Finding what he was looking for, Doctor Trent pulled out three separate x-ray photos and laid them on the bed in front of Stuart.

'We did some brain scans when you were brought in. Most people at this point would be in a coma, but to everyone's complete shock and amazement, you weren't. In fact, for a second we were worried you were dead already until we took your pulse,' said Doctor Trent as he pointed his finger at each x-ray in turn.

'Wow. What happened, then?' said Stuart with raised eyebrows.

'In this sort of situation we would expect broken bones, a few cracked ribs, and possibly even internal bleeding. But the worst thing that we found on you was a slight bump on your head,' said Doctor Trent.

Stuart chuckled, as he had a fleeting image of slamming into the side of the ambulance at the scene of the crash. 'I must be stronger than I look, doctor,' said Stuart, smiling slightly at this last remark.

Doctor Trent relaxed a little as he readied himself to ask another question. 'You don't mind me asking these things, do you, Mr Robson?' asked Doctor Trent.

'Of course I don't. Anything to help the medical profession,' answered Stuart, who had been looking at the x-ray photos whilst Doctor Trent had taken a break in his lecture.

'You don't think that your Asperger's could somehow be responsible for the quick recovery on your body, do you?' asked Doctor Trent.

'I don't think so. Autism is something that affects the brain rather than the rest of my body. I remember waking up and finding that I wasn't wearing my crash helmet,' said Stuart.

Doctor Trent started to explain again, with Stuart giving him his full and undivided attention. 'The paramedic first on the scene determined that it was safe to remove your crash helmet because there were no signs of neck injury,' said Doctor Trent. He gave Stuart a look as if to say, 'Don't worry, these people are professionals.'

'I saw her,' said Stuart suddenly, not meaning to come out with the last sentence.

'Saw who?' said Doctor Trent, looking around the room.

'The angel. Her name is Sophie,' said Stuart.

'That makes sense. You kept saying the word "Sophie" over and over again when you were brought in,' said Doctor Trent. Stuart thought back to what he had seen and heard whilst in the white emptiness he had been so convinced was his trusty mind box.

'Your head will never forget, but your heart will always forgive,' said Stuart as the image of Emily Green's face with its shoulder-length blonde hair and sparkling brown eyes swam before his vision again.

'No!' exclaimed Stuart so loudly that a nurse walking past in the corridor outside looked through the window in alarm.

'What's wrong?' said Doctor Trent as he recoiled slightly, wondering what was happening.

'Nothing. I thought I saw something,' said Stuart, brushing his utterance aside like some sort of pointless answer in a school exam.

'You know, that's not as uncommon as it sounds,' said Doctor Trent, who had put his hands together in his lap, thinking hard.

'You haven't got any sort of medication, have you, Doc?' said Stuart.

Doctor Trent only laughed and replied, 'Oh no. You've only been given a drip feed but nothing else like that. What I meant to say is, a person often experiences a rush of emotion and visions before they die, which culminates in some people saying that they see their life flash before their eyes.'

'I like your thinking, doctor, but I know I didn't see my life flashing before my eyes. This was something else,' replied Stuart, now feeling that he was about to go into great detail about what had really happened after the collision. Doctor Trent seemed to be the edge of his seat with interest as Stuart began to relay the story of what he had seen and heard after the impact. When Stuart had finished talking, Doctor Trent leaned back in his chair looking wide-eyed and amazed at the piece of mental software that Stuart had created.

'Let me get this straight. You're saying that your condition is effectively a sub consciousness that lives inside your mind all the time?' said Doctor Trent as Stuart nodded his agreement.

'My God, you're incredible,' replied Doctor Trent.

'What's incredible?' asked Stuart.

'It's just you as a person; you've managed to mentally create a whole new way of thinking in the development of mental software and survive a motorcycle traffic collision which should have been fatal if not put you in a coma at the very least. The medical science board are going to have a field day,' said Doctor Trent, standing up and grabbing hold of his notes while trying not to look excited at this medical breakthrough that he'd discovered.

'With your permission, Mr Robson, I'd like to take a blood sample for analysis, just so we can eliminate any further problems that we might have missed,' said Doctor Trent, opening the door and calling the nurse over.

'Of course, I'm all right with that,' said Stuart as the nurse came in, straightening his pillows and clipping a new water bag to the drip feeder.

'We'll move you to the blood unit by the end of today to extract the samples, and then we can sign the discharge papers' said the nurse as Doctor Trent exited the room, leaving Stuart to his thoughts yet again. Had he really just made medical history, or was this just standard-issue procedure for a doctor's visit?

And so it was later that day Stuart found himself queuing outside in the corridor to the blood donors' department, as Doctor Trent had requested. When he was finally admitted Stuart wasn't sure how much blood he would have to give them. The on-duty nurse told him not to worry too much, as they usually only extracted small amounts for medical purposes. To her complete surprise, Stuart managed to give well over six test tubes before getting up and leaving, still as fit and well as he had been when he came in.

Back at home from the hospital for the first time in well over a week, Stuart recounted his experience of the crash in great detail for what felt like the thousandth time, making sure to leave out the part where he went inside of his mind box and met Sophie for the first time.

'The police charged the lorry driver, you know – driving without due care and attention, I think they said,' replied Abigail as Stuart tucked into his dinner with the rest of his family. This was his favourite sausages and mash with gravy.

'I should think so too; that blind maniac could have killed you. The driver at the wheel of the people carrier was a bit shaken, but they're okay now,' said David.

Stuart commented, 'At least I'm in the club now – first bike crash and all that.'

David grinned to himself, admiring his eldest son's optimism, but Abigail looked shocked and astounded at this last statement. 'Mum, look at Guy Martin on the telly, the one who does all those TT races on the Isle of Man. He's had loads of crashes, and he just shakes it off like it never happened,' said Stuart, responding to Abigail's last expression.

Abigail looked ready to answer back at this point but suddenly felt a hand on her arm. David moved across to her and gave her an expression which quite plainly said, 'Drop it.'

'Why did you stop me earlier? Why didn't you just let me talk to him?' said Abigail hours later whilst the pair of them sat up reading in their bed.

'Because I wanted to talk to him as well, but I've realised now that the crash he had wasn't his fault,' said David, lowering the magazine on vintage tractors he had been reading to look at Abigail properly.

'I don't want to see my son killed chasing some crazy ambition. He's Stuart Robson, not Donald Campbell,' said Abigail.

'I want to be honest with you here, Abigail. Stuart has an ability, a talent even, and a fascination with driving and mechanics that none of us will even be able to begin to understand,' said David.

Abigail was suddenly taken back to the meeting that had taken place just after Stuart had started school at the age of five. Little bits of the meeting jumped out of her, like 'struggling socially' and 'unable to live independently'.

'Just let him do what he does. You never know. If he wins this race, it could really open some doors for his life and his understanding of the world,' said David, bringing Abigail back to reality after she'd been lost in her own mind space.

'What did we do to deserve this?' said Abigail.

David put his magazine down again with a sigh. 'We didn't do anything wrong. Anyway, Stuart is the one who has to live with autism twenty-four hours a day, not us; it's him we should feel sorry for.'

Chapter Fifteen

Thunderbolt to Pole Position

'Night, darling,' said David, giving Abigail a small kiss on the check before turning over to switch off the bedside lamp, plunging the whole room into darkness. With the British touring car championship coming up at the Silverstone raceway at the end of the month, Team Robson had their work cut out to get everything ready for the race itself. A few weeks had passed since the Harley crash, but even that hadn't stopped Stuart from coming to the qualifying stages to get Team Robson into the race itself. The final team was decided as David holding the captain's position with Stuart as head mechanic as well as a driver. Ben was to be the secondary driver next to Stuart, with Adam heading up race commentary control and computer readouts to be relayed throughout the whole team during the race.

All in all, the entire team would be run like a military unit, with each person knowing their responsibility and role within the team. Thunderbolt itself had been kept under a sheet since its repair a few weeks ago to hide it away from prying cameras and freelance journalists as well as petrol-heads from motoring magazines. All this was to be in vain, however. As Ben pressed the button to raise the main pit shutter door up, a small crowd of journalists descended on Stuart and the rest of Team Robson.

David stepped forward to address the crowd. 'Good morning, everyone. My name is David. I'm the Team Robson captain, and our car is the BMW 3-Series race car, which has been given the name Thunderbolt.'

Stuart hung slightly back in the background, hoping not to be seen too much, but the cameras got there first.

'What role are you in the team, sir?' said a reporter as the camera's attention turned to Stuart.

'Ah yes, allow me to introduce my eldest son, Stuart, who is our lead driver and will be doing the first two-hour stint in the race,' said David before Stuart could get a word out.

A few flashes went off as Stuart attempted to smile for the camera, feeling stretched to the breaking point at the intense level of social activity all round him. After a few minutes, which felt to Stuart like a lifetime, the crowd of reporters broke apart, moving on to the other racers.

'Hey, Dad, I'm going to take a look up the line and see what we're up against,' said Stuart as David headed back for the motorhome at the back of the pit garage.

'See you in a bit,' said David as Stuart made his way up the line, looking at the other competitors.

The other pit lanes were also a hive of activity as the other teams prepared their cars for the main race the very next day. There were many cars, including two very high-end, state-of-the-art Aston Martin DB-RS9s, which were the racing versions of the standard DB9 road built super car. Stuart's idea of heaven was being around all of the racing cars in their highly polished state. Being a mainly home-built car, Thunderbolt was in a separate category for kit cars. He turned around to head back towards the Robson pit garage and accidently walked into something quite solid.

'Oh, I'm so sorry,' said Stuart, a little dazed, as he looked at the stranger he had just walked into.

'Hello, Stuart,' said a familiar voice. Stuart looked up to see Rick Green standing in front of him.

'Rick, hi. What are you doing here?' said Stuart in surprise, holding out a hand to shake Rick's.

'Having a look at your shiny new race car. Very nice, I might say,' said Rick.

'Thanks. What do you think?' said Stuart as Rick smiled.

'I like it, although it seems you have a bit more of a soft spot for my eldest daughter,' said Rick as Stuart gulped heavily. Now he was going to get it. He had felt bad enough when Emily himself had turned him away for asking her out.

'Don't look so worried, Stu. When I heard about it I almost laughed out loud with joy,' said Rick as the two of them started to walk back towards the Robson pit garage. 'Between you and me, Emily is quite happy with her boyfriend, but I do think it was nice of you to do those things for her. And deep down she really did appreciate it,' said Rick.

Stuart seemed relieved as they stood side by side, leaning on the rail which was the boundary to the race track. 'I feel so stupid, though. I mean to say that I love her, I really do, but I'm going to have to live with the fact that we can never be together in a relationship for the rest of our lives,' said Stuart.

Rick gave a little sigh and turned to look at him. 'I just want to offer you a little advice. Don't stop seeing Emily completely, but still talk to her as you would to a very good friend. Good luck in the race tomorrow.' Rick clapped Stuart on the shoulder and disappeared in the crowd before Stuart could say another word. Stuart continued to look out at the racetrack for the rest of the day until the sun had set completely before making his way back to the Robson pit garage.

He'd been mulling over the words that Rick had spoken to him earlier that day and had come to the conclusion that it was a long shot at most. How exactly was he supposed to be a friend to Emily and not feel a powerful desire to kiss her every ten minutes because of her pure beauty and attractiveness?

'What would you do, Sophie?' asked Stuart as he poured himself a drink at the sink inside the motorhome ten minutes later.

'Personally, if I was a man I would propose to her. But that seems to be out of the question right now,' said Sophie as she appeared at his side wearing her usual knee-length bright blue dress with matching high heels. Stuart almost jumped out of his skin, not being quite used to this sudden apparition.

'What's so scary?' asked Sophie, sitting down on the bed before fixing him with one of those curious looks.

'It's okay, Sophie. It's just I'm not used to you coming in like that,' said Stuart, smiling at her as she grinned back. A silence filled the next few minutes. Stuart turned to gaze out of the window at the now-dark racetrack lit with only the lights of the other motorhomes. Even Sophie seemed lost for words as she turned her head this way and that to figure out what to say to Stuart. Even her female wisdom may not have helped him at this point.

'I'm sorry,' said Stuart to break the silence.

'Whatever for? It's not your fault that Emily isn't here with you,' replied Sophie, a little confused.

'No, it's not that. It's just – I'm sorry you have to be, you know, locked up in my head all the time like a mental prisoner,' said Stuart.

'I'm not a prisoner; I never have been. I'm always there for you, and we're always going to be there for one another, aren't we?' replied Sophie with a small laugh. Stuart grinned back, thinking back to Emily's good looks back in the pub when she had taken him on that practice date in what felt like another lifetime.

'I mean to say, you were the one who created me. You did it by accident, I'll admit, but who says that all accidents have to be bad ones?' said Sophie.

The side door of the motorhome suddenly opened as David stuck his head in. 'You should get some rest. It's going to be a long one tomorrow,' said David as Stuart looked round at the bed. Sophie, of course, had vanished from view.

David frowned slightly. 'What's up?' he said as Stuart shook his head.

'Nothing, I'm fine,' said Stuart. David closed the door, allowing Stuart to switch out the light on the ceiling. As he lay down where Sophie had been sitting he felt a slight chill, as if a consciousness had been lying there only moment before – and maybe even still lay there.

Tomorrow was the big moment for Stuart and the team: the national twelve-hour endurance touring car championship race at Silverstone racetrack. Almost as if a film were playing in his head, Stuart imagined driving at breakneck speed through the chequered flag as the racing commentator proclaimed, 'I give you Thunderbolt'. The crowd was cheering its approval as Stuart and the rest of the team celebrated by standing on the finishing podium to hoist up the winning cup. But for now, that was only a dream. Or was it?

Chapter Sixteen

The Race Begins

At dawn, the Silverstone race track was still and calm. The sounds of birds filled early risers' ears before they were replaced with the sounds of air guns, trolley jacks, and reversing lorry sirens. In the Team Robson pit box, Thunderbolt was propped up on two trolley jacks. Stuart, unable to sleep due to anticipation of the race ahead, rummaged around underneath making sure all of the parts were secure and working properly.

'Stuart, what you doing? The race doesn't start for another two hours yet,' asked David, yawning. He had just come out of the team's motorhome pulling on his racing suit.

'I'm doing all of the vehicle checks. Why are you in a racing suit' said Stuart, a little taken aback.

'I had a long, hard thought about it last night and decided that I wanted to have the chance to drive Thunderbolt in the race,' said David, smiling and standing proud for a second.

'But Dad, you've not been doing any of the track day try-outs or qualifying. You're not even down on the list of drivers to race,' said Stuart. He stood up, wondering if this was a good idea.

'Hey, come on, Stu. I was the one giving the financial backing on this, and my company name is stamped all over these vehicles and on that car. It would be a bit stupid not to do it,' said David, picking up the crash helmet as Stuart wiped his hands on a bit of rag laying on the bonnet. David disappeared outside, leaving Stuart to run his hand over the paintwork, thinking, *Ready to go, old girl.*

As the sun started to come up fully in the sky, the stands filled up with spectators carrying everything from digital cameras to buckets of popcorn, ready for another action-packed race at Silverstone. Back in the motorhome, Stuart had swapped his boiler suit for a full racing driver's suit, which read 'Robson Transport Limited' along with his name, which Stuart had topped off with a set of captain's stripes across the shoulders. Abigail Robson was brushing him down as usual, being her OCD self about finding dust particles in the most unexpected of places.

'Mum, I'm fine,' said Stuart with a quick glance at the look on her face, which was a mixture of happiness and worry.

'I know you are. I'm just worried, that's all,' said Abigail, looking Stuart straight in the eye.

'Mum, the doctors gave me a full bill of health and told me I was fit to drive again. So really, don't worry about me,' said Stuart, taking her hand and giving it a little squeeze.

'You almost died in that motorcycle collision. Heaven forbid I ever let you near one of those again,' said Abigail.

But as she said this, Stuart let out a slight laugh. 'Fat chance of that! I'm eyeing up my next bike already. I was going to use the race winnings to buy it. I was going to call it "Black Bonnie," after ....'

Stuart broke off and bowed his head. As he did so, Emily's face swam clearly in front of his eyes.

'After what?' asked Abigail with a small smile. But it was almost as if she had guessed, for when Stuart looked up her eyes were level with his. *Where's Sophie when you need her?* thought Stuart, almost knowing that a reprimand was only seconds away.

'She's gone, Stu, and she was never your girlfriend in the first place' said Abigail firmly as she finished brushing him down before standing back to admire her handiwork.

'Now I do believe you've got a race to win,' said Abigail before Stuart could speak again. Standing proud and tall, Stuart squared his shoulders and stood to attention as Abigail slid his racing crash helmet under his arm. Turning on the spot like a soldier on parade, he marched straight out of the motorhome's open door towards the pit where Thunderbolt stood ready to go. David was there by the computer with a pair of headphones over his head listening to the commentary now coming from the main stand. Stuart tapped him on the shoulder as David turned to look.

'Ready,' mouthed Stuart, knowing David would not be able to hear him over the noise of the other cars.

David gave the thumbs-up sign in his direction before turning back to the screen to monitor the streams of information that were coming through. As Stuart stepped up to Thunderbolt he found his team standing around him waiting for their instructions. Stuart pointed his hand outside in an almost military fashion, as a captain would command a ship, and the team understood his meaning exactly: 'Let's do this'.

The whole racing team consisted of six people who covered multiple roles within the pits. Stuart and Ben were the marked drivers on the racing rota, which David had added himself to afterwards, much to Stuart's surprise and wonder. David was marked as the team's captain and was pit crew chief in charge of radios and lap relays when not out on the track. This placed him in an ideal position to monitor the other drivers and their individual progress during the race as well keep a constant stream on commentary to whoever was driving Thunderbolt on the track. Ben had volunteered to refuel and tyre change when not out on the track. This was officially the job of Adam, also a lifelong friend of Stuart, who for a number of weeks now had been taking hits and tips from Stuart on how to work air guns in order to change all of the tyres in less than two minutes, which was his record to date. In a race, speed and timing were everything.

Finally there were Abigail and Edward. Both had made it plain to Stuart and David that they had no knowledge or interest in racing at all but, in the spirit of teamwork, would be in charge of catering and general serving of tea and biscuits. Edward, who was a mechanical engineer by trade, had said that he could repair any parts that went wrong during the race, so he had brought his van full of machinery tools with him.

As his team dispersed, Stuart managed to squeeze himself into the small cockpit, which was now even smaller thanks to the new racing seat which had been fitted for safety reasons. He inserted the key into a small white box by the side of the steering wheel and turned it. A small humming sound came from inside the car as all the dials and switches lit up, ready to run. The engine fired, growling its newly rebuilt and revamped Audi eight-litre V10 engine. Smiling to himself, Stuart allowed a few light presses of the accelerator pedal, listening to its beating thumps, which made the whole car vibrate.

'Radio check,' said Stuart, sliding his crash helmet onto his head before plugging himself into the intercom system on the cars system.

'Radio check reading you loud and clear. Good luck out there, Stu,' said David as Thunderbolt rolled out of the pit into the service lane, ready to enter the main track for the starting grid. As Stuart rolled down the service lane he saw the eyes of other teams on him.

This being the official UK touring car championship race, all of the cars entered were standard-built road cars with racing equipment fitted to them. There were BMWs, Audis, Alfa Romeos, and even a few Aston Martin DB RS9s. As a tribute to David Robson turning fifty the same year, it had been decided that Thunderbolt's racing number would be fifty.

Once Stuart had left the pit lane, he merged onto the track and was instantly up behind a pace car. This particular pace car was a top-of-the-range Mercedes-Benz SLS AMG sports car with its amber flashing beacons and the words 'Race Marshall' written on the side. 'Hey Stu, I think you should have a listen to this,' said David, coming through on the radio.

As he finished speaking, what sounded like commentary of the race started coming though. 'Now the cars are starting to come out onto the track for their show laps. In front of the queue, right behind the pace car, is number fifty known as Thunderbolt, driven by Mr Stuart Robson of Robson Transport Limited in Hertfordshire.'

As the commentator finished his speech, Stuart held his arm as high as it would go out of the window and started waving to the crowds of spectators that now lined the track. The crowd cheered and clapped its approval as Stuart started to move from side to side, trying to warm his tyres. He was soon joined by the other race cars that were filtering out from the pit lane as they started to take their places on the grid.

Stuart, who'd done his best during the qualifying stages, had got to fifth place on the grid, right behind the two Aston Martin DB-RS9s, which held the third and fourth positions. The second position was a BMW M3 series which was driven under the name of Hogarth Houseware Limited. The first position was being held by an Alfa Romeo GTV six sport which was under the name of Preston Plumbing. At the back of the stands Rick stared through a pair of binoculars looking at all the competitors. He soon picked out Thunderbolt near the front of the grid and gave a wave over the crowd before realising that Stuart couldn't have seen him due to his distance.

Emily, who wanted to come, had decided instead to remain at home and watched coverage of the race on the TV. She had been worried that possibly seeing Stuart there might have caused him to lose focus during the race, especially after the meeting they had in the barn a few weeks earlier. As she saw Thunderbolt appear on the television screen she felt a tear start to come to her eye. Why, why did she have to tell him in that way that she was already in a relationship? Their conversation had already caused a near-fatal motorcycle crash on that dark country road. Stuart had been besotted by her and never said anything to her about his unrequited love. She felt guilty about admitting it now, but it seemed that Stuart had been there all the time. She'd not taken him seriously. Against all of the odds, despite his social awkwardness and complete craziness, he wasn't really a bad or mad person at all.

All that had come from the whole situation was that it would have put Stuart off getting into a relationship ever again. Reaching for the remote control, she turned the volume up a little before curling herself up the sofa to keep warm, trying to keep her mind off of the whole terrible business.

Back at Silverstone the other competitors had all taken their places on the grid as the commentators finished their statements about the teams and racing cars. As suddenly as they stopped speaking, the red lights appeared above the racing gantry, telling all drivers to get ready. As there were no amber lights, each driver was on edge for action waiting for the green. Engines started to rev up, and the odd flame spurted out from the exhausts.

Stuart pushed the accelerator a little and felt the engine give a growl of pistons. He saw the rev needle move from tick-over speed of fifteen hundred revs to four thousand and back again. Another pair of red lights appeared below the first. He gripped the steering wheel, bracing himself for the green light above the gantry. In the next second the red lights vanished to be replaced with a single row of greens. There was a blast from an air horn as the crowd cheered its approval. In the next second the air was filled with screeching tyres and high revving engines as all of the competing race cars shot forward off the line. The clock above the gantry started to count down the time till the end of the race: eleven hours and fifty-nine minutes to go until the final chequered flag. This was it; the race had begun.

Chapter Seventeen

Full Power

Stuart was thrust back into the seat, only just keeping hold of the steering wheel, as the full power of Thunderbolt's V10 modified engine was unleashed. It shot straight between the two Aston Martin DB RS9s, which divided sideways, not wanting to be hit by what felt like the almost nuclear-powered race car.

'And they're off! Wow, Team Robson have jumped two places in the first few seconds, and look at that racer go. Driver Stuart Robson is on to a winner here,' came the commentary over the loudspeaker as the crowd cheered and clapped their approval.

Back in the pits David was speaking to Stuart on his radio set, watching live pictures from the computer screen in front of him. 'Go on, my son. Those DB9s are right on your tail; stay outside and you should take them by surprise.'

'Ten four, Dad. Stay outside,' said Stuart, turning into the first corner and feeling the back end of the car start to kick out as the two DB9s revved up. Then they slowed down behind Stu as they were pelted with bits of gravel being picked up under Thunderbolt's wheels. Counter-steering a little, Thunderbolt drifted for a second before straightening up again for the second corner. It was a good thing the wishbone racing suspension had been reinforced with extra plates, as it was creaking slightly with Thunderbolt entering the second corner on a hairpin bend doing in excess of 60 mph. In his excitement, Stuart after exiting the second corner had left a huge gap open for the two DB9s, which had still been behind him since the start. They soon took advantage of this, shooting through the open gap with a burst of speed.

There was a collective sigh from the crowd as one of the DB9s overtook him and came within inches of hitting the side of Thunderbolt. In the stands Ricky pulled a face, looking through his binoculars.

'I should be down there,' said Rick to himself, placing the binoculars back to his eyes.

'Wow, that could have been nasty. Team Robson must be feeling the heat now from Team AM,' said the commentator.

Back in the pits, Ben had joined in the commentary on the team radio. 'Stuart, we've got the finishing straight coming up soon. You can show that DB9 who's boss, right?' said Ben with a quick look at David, who pulled a face and crossed his fingers. After all, Aston Martin DB9s were supercars and probably had a lot more power than Thunderbolt did.

Less a minute later, it seemed, the cars rounded the final corner and were on the main straight. Stuart was now in fourth position, having been taken by a Lotus Elise and the BMW M3 which had been in second place to start.

'All right, Stu, full power. Punch it,' said David as Stuart, unwilling, floored the accelerator pedal. Something which sounded like a missile exploding erupted from the exhaust as Thunderbolt shot forward, overtaking the two DB9s from the start. Stuart watched the speedometer start to climb: 130, 150, 180. As the needle reached the 190-mph mark, he felt the steering wheel start to vibrate. Could he make 200 mph on the straight before the first corner again? It was at this point that Stuart passed the Team Robson pit so fast it was almost as if a Formula One car had rocketed past them.

Abigail jumped in shock as the sound of all ten of the car's cylinders nearly exploded under the pressure. 'Was that –' said Abigail to the team, but they didn't seem to hear her. All of them had placed their hands over their ears due to the noise coming from less than ten meters away.

'Good god,' said Rick back in the stands, failing to keep Thunderbolt in his sights as it was so quick.

'Stu, that is an Audi V10 engine, isn't it? It's not got some nuclear device on board or something?' asked David over the radio.

The reply from Stuart was very quick. 'No, I just switched on the two turbo chargers I've got under here; that gave it some kick.' It certainly had. Thunderbolt and Team Robson were back in pole position.

According to the watch Stuart had fixed to the steering wheel for time checks, he'd been running for nearly two hours. It was time for a driver change. Almost as if they had waiting for it, the whole team scrambled out to meet Thunderbolt as if mobilising a pair of fighter jets for take-off. Screeching his brakes a little in the pit lane, Ben dropped the small stop sign in front of Thunderbolt, and the whole team got to work. Adam and Ben went to work on the tyres as David grabbed his crash helmet from the side before sliding into the driver's seat. Stuart closed the door on him. As Edward Robson fuelled up the tank the whole crew backed off, having replaced the old worn-out tyres with brand-new ones. They knew full well that every second in the pit could be the difference between winning and losing.

Giving the thumbs-up, David spun the rear wheels on Thunderbolt. Tyre smoke floated up as it shot forward, heading for the pit lane exit back onto the track.

'That was a good run you had. It said on there your fastest lap time was just under two minutes,' said Abigail. She handed Stuart a freshly made cup of tea, which he gulped down in one go.

'Thanks, Mum,' he replied, handing the cup back to her. Ben gave him the thumbs-up from the computer. Stuart sat down next to him to monitor the screen and listen to the radio commentary now coming from the main control box up in the stands. With the hours ticking by, Team Robson climbed up place after place on the grid, taking everything and everyone by storm. The commentators couldn't believe what they were seeing.

Although they were a first-time team at their first championship race, nothing and nobody seemed to be able to beat Stuart Robson and his Asperger's-built touring car. Alternating between David, Ben, and Stuart, Team Robson had climbed up two places, lost four, and then gained another two again. This meant they were in third place, right behind the two Aston Martin DB-RS9s – which, however hard Team Robson tried, were keeping Thunderbolt just behind them. When Stuart pitted for the end of his second driving stint, he nearly kicked the rubbish bin standing up against the wall in frustration. This time it was Ben's turn in Thunderbolt. He jumped in and did another two-hour stint before coming back in and reporting that the two DB-RS9s were holding him back.

With two hours left to go, it was time for the final stint. 'This is all yours, Stu,' said David. Stuart did as he was instructed, taking Thunderbolt out onto the track for the very last time. Once again he climbed into Thunderbolt and sped away out onto the track, where he soon made up the ground lost whilst being in the pits. The other cars just seemed to fall away into the distance as Stuart caught up with the lead Aston Martin DB-RS9s, which still held the first and second places.

Up until this point, Stuart had refrained from using his mind box abilities. He felt this would have been cheating; after all, none of the other racing drivers could use what he had in his mind. Going forward into another corner, Stuart spotted a gap and decided to just go for it.

Chapter Eighteen

You Win My Love

To his complete surprise, Thunderbolt snuck past, making the lead Aston Martin momentarily stamp on its brakes.

'Yes! Go, Stu, go!' shouted David in the pits as the rest of the team cheered and clapped one another on the backs. After being ranked between sixth and third during the whole race, Thunderbolt and Team Robson were now in first position for the first time.

'Wow, an incredible move by Team Robson, taking the lead cars by storm. With only eight minutes of racing left, the three leaders are neck and neck,' came the race commentary over the loudspeakers beside the track.

Back on the track, Stuart gripped the steering wheel hard as he clipped the gravel by the side of the track. One of the Aston Martins grabbed first positon from right under Thunderbolt's nose.

'Don't lose focus, Stu. You can do this. Let's show that Aston who's boss and get first place back,' said David in an encouraging voice over the radio to Stuart, who felt a little pang of annoyance at the sudden overtake.

'I'm running out of time. He's got my outside and is holding a strong position,' replied Stuart.

But a sudden voice brought him crashing back to earth and made his senses sore. 'Yes you can. You know you can.' It was the voice of Emily Green, who had decided that she couldn't bear sitting at home any longer and wanted to be in the thick of the action itself. She had made way her north as quickly as possible to be there to witness the end of the race.

'Emily? My God, what are you doing here?' said Stuart in shock as he realised who it was on the end of the radio headset.

'I was wrong about you, Stu. Don't just try and win this for the team. Win this for me as well,' said Emily in a reassuring voice.

David smiled at her. They both stood by the race computer monitoring Stuart's progress as Thunderbolt and the two Aston Martins rounded the final corner onto the straight.

'It's show time. Engaging maximum thunder!' said Stuart, punching his foot down hard on the accelerator pedal. In that fraction of a second everything seemed to move in slow motion. Stuart turned his head to the left to see the lead Aston Martin draw level with him as they raced towards the finish line for what was going to be the final lap. Everything then returned to normal speed again as what felt like the force of a supersonic fighter jet rushed through the cockpit.

Stuart was thrown back into his chair as Thunderbolt shot forward, leaving the Aston Martins way behind him. The team in the pit garage felt the force of Thunderbolt hurtle past them at a speed of over 200 mph. The fences on the side of the racetrack rattled at the force of the speeding cars. Stuart punched his fist into the air, having finally gotten Thunderbolt over the 200 mph barrier for the first time. He entered the first corner again at speed with the two Aston Martins right on his tail. The rear spoiler pushed the back into the ground, causing a little bit of tyre smoke as Thunderbolt soldiered on. Using his rear view mirror, Stuart saw the Aston Martins start to gain some ground on him, but it was lost on the finishing straight.

Back in the pit garage, the whole team held its breath. This was the moment of truth. After twelve hours of racing, it all came down to this crucial moment. Could Stuart hold his nerve and actually win this race that they'd all dreamed and worked so hard on for so long? After a few tense minutes the three main leaders emerged around the final corner on the finishing straight. The two Aston Martins had once again taken the lead and were doing their best to stop Thunderbolt from getting through to victory. In the crowd Rick had his binoculars glued to his eyes, watching the tense actions of the cars on the track with great interest.

'Come on, Stu! You can do it,' said Rick as he managed to lock onto Thunderbolt just behind the two Aston Martins.

As Thunderbolt went on the attack, accelerating hard, the two Astons closed ranks to stop him from passing. But in their eagerness to stop Stuart, they had failed to spot a gap which had opened between them and the wire fence on the pit lane. Realising the error too late, one of the Astons attempted to block Stuart but hit the pit lane wall. With a loud crash from the impact it skidded away, allowing Thunderbolt to power onto victory over the finish line. The marshals were waving their chequered flags high in the air, signalling the end of the race. The stands erupted with cheers and clapping as the now slightly smashed-up Aston Martin came to a stop by the wall. The other cars crossed the line in a mixture of surprise and confusion at the amazing outcome.

Team Robson erupted with cheers and whoops, slapping one another on the backs. David and Abigail hugged one another as Ben and Adam punched their fists into the air. Edward made an American army salute with his hand, and Emily felt a tear start to come to her eye at the overwhelming joy of seeing Stuart win the best event in his lifetime. The delighted commentator reported the victory for Team Robson of Robson Transport Limited.

Stuart, meanwhile, had started doing a few doughnuts on the track in a sort of victory celebration before speeding off round the track on what was known to many as the victory lap of honour. As the ambulance crews pulled the driver of the crashed Aston Martin to safety, Stuart gave him a small wave as if to say, 'Sorry about the car'.

The driver nodded in acknowledgment before the paramedics carted him off to the waiting ambulance for some much-needed medical checks. When Thunderbolt finally came to a stop outside the Team Robson pit garage, Stuart flung open the door and was immediately pounced upon by the whole team. But winning this race was only a lifelong ambition. His greatest challenge to date was in fact winning over the love of the beautiful Miss Emily Green, whose eyes met his as he pulled himself out from inside Thunderbolt, victorious.

'That's my boy!' said David as Abigail ran forward and hugged Stuart around the shoulders.

'Way to go, mate,' said Ben and Adam in unison as they patted Stuart on the shoulder for a job well done.

Chapter Nineteen

The Legend Begins

'I think we should let him breathe, guys,' said Emily in a jokey voice. She smiled broadly at Stuart, who grinned back at her in thanks for being there when he needed her the most.

'You know, I'm really sorry if I ever doubted you, Emily,' said Stuart. Emily grinned with happiness again, thinking back to the incident in the barn where Stuart had got down on one knee and proposed to be her boyfriend.

'I thought you were an oddball at first, Stu, but I guess it's always the oddballs that make the biggest mark on the world,' said Emily, trying her best to be a comfort to Stuart rather than an aggressor.

'You win my love and make my motor run,' said Stuart as Emily looked confused.

'Is that a song?' she asked as Stuart smiled again at the sound of his favourite country singer.

'It's by Shania Twain, from one of her country albums – all about racing cars, funnily enough,' replied Stuart. They made their way back towards the motorhome. The after party to celebrate winning the race at Silverstone was only the start of things for Stuart and the rest of Team Robson. Abigail, in secret from everybody else, had made a celebration fruitcake to prepare for that day's win. But before they could all dive in and eat it, the paparazzi had descended upon them and began bombarding the whole team with questions about their victory in the race. David, of course, did his usual and went to greet them to save Stuart having to be put into a sociably awkward situation. But Stuart knew he couldn't hide forever, so, still buzzing from the win, he made his way to the winning podium to collect the shining silver trophy from the race marshals.

The crowd erupted in cheers and clapping as a triumphant-looking Stuart hoisted the trophy into the air above his head before being showered, in traditional style, by a fountain of champagne and flowers with a wreath round his neck. Stuart's distant dream had become a solid reality.

In the weeks following the victory at Silverstone, reporters from all over the country turned up at the Robson Limited Headquarters wanting to speak to Stuart, David and the others on how it went for them, what was going through their minds at the time of the win, and of course the extraordinary car which had won the race. Stuart, of course, was in his element, showing Thunderbolt draped in the car-sized UK flag he'd bought using his winning money. The modified Audi V10 turbo-charged engine sat in a glass case on the bench in the corner, having been taken out and rebuilt after the race.

Each day Stuart and David would go home to find mountains of letters from car magazines wanting to exhibit Thunderbolt in on their front cover. One man who lived in Northumberland sent a letter asking for the original designs, as he wanted to build a replica model of Thunderbolt.

'The legend begins,' said Abigail jokingly as she made tea for the pair of them. Stuart sat once again at the kitchen table replying to the letters and Facebook messages he had been sent over the last couple of weeks from the now long list of Team Robson admirers.

Putting his pen down flush with the letter he was writing, he stared out of the window at the closed barn where all of his hard work had been done over the last couple of months.

'Go on, then, but five minutes only. This cup of tea won't stay warm,' said Abigail, seeing Stuart's gaze.

'Thanks, Mum,' said Stuart. He raced out the door across the yard before sliding open the two brown double doors. Thunderbolt gleamed in the light coming through from outside the doors as he ran his hand along the bodywork, thinking back to the moment Thunderbolt crossed the line. He recalled the cheers and roars of the crowds as the other cars raced around the track at breakneck speed.

'She did you proud, didn't she?' said Sophie, who had appeared by Stuart's side in her usual state of being visible to none but himself.

'Yes, she did. She did us all proud,' said Stuart, not turning round but continuing to look, unfazed, into the rims on the front and rear wheels. He was getting used to Sophie being a part of his life. He had been meaning to ask other people if they sensed Sophie's presence, but they would probably think he was daft.

Abigail's voice brought Stuart back to his senses. He made his way back towards the farmhouse, giving Thunderbolt one last look before pushing the doors to and bolting them shut.

Chapter Twenty

Black Bonnie

Six whole months had passed since the race at Silverstone, and Stuart had once again gone to cleaning up after himself, being a little on the OCD side of life. The shiny Silverstone trophy that Stuart had won during the touring car championship race was kept in the downstairs living room locked away in a cupboard, only to be put on display during social gatherings to save it getting dirty. His bedroom was the usual organized mess, now a little redecorated with a new coat of blue paint on the walls and a very large A1-sized picture of Stuart leaning up against the Thunderbolt touring car. The title underneath read, 'Silverstone championship race winner, Team Robson, with the BMW M3 Series race car Thunderbolt'.

With his bedroom sorted out, Stuart took a trip across town to Emily's house to check up on her. The last time he had seen her was about a week after the race at Silverstone. Emily had been offered an exciting new job in a local government office, which meant that she spent a lot of time working and was hardly ever at home.

As Stuart went for the door knocker the front door suddenly opened, leaving him with one fist in the air. Julie stood there with a smile on her face. 'Good morning, Mrs Green. I have to report that your front door has disappeared,' said Stuart in an attempt to crack a joke, still holding his fist in the air.

'Yes, I opened it, Mr Robson,' said Julie. As Stuart put his hand down, another face appeared at Julie's shoulder. Stuart grinned at the sight.

'I think it best if I leave you two alone now,' said Julie as she retreated, letting Emily come to the front to be with Stuart.

'Hi. I bought you these,' said Stuart, holding out a bunch of flowers to Emily.

'Aww, thank you, Stu,' said Emily, who grinned appreciatively and placed them down on the small table just inside of the door.

'How have you been?' asked Emily as she tried to fill in the gap of Stuart's present of flowers with something easy to say.

'I've been okay. Life's been the same, really,' said Stuart, trying to sound normal. But Emily was too quick for him.

'You miss me, don't you?' she said as Stuart attempted to avert his eyes from her and the question that he had been so worried she would ask him.

Emily's pure beauty and kindness had always been of great comfort to Stuart, but he never knew why. 'I don't understand it. Every time I try and go anywhere near a member of the opposite sex, I either become a mental nervous wreck or they just slip away like I'm some sort of contaminated creature,' said Stuart, trying to keep his voice level. 'I always loved you, Emily. You know, I never forgot you at all, even when you turned me away.'

Emily sighed a little. 'I always thought that you had some sort of feelings towards me, but I just didn't know how to break it to you about my relationship,' said Emily.

Stuart's expression remained the same. 'Why is it that all the good-looking girls have to have boyfriends, and why is it always so hard to get one to like you?' he asked as Emily let out a little laugh.

'Aww, that's so sweet of you too say that. So you're not a robot then. You do have feelings,' said Emily. Stuart seemed a little flustered by this last statement.

'But you get everything, and you don't have to do anything to get it – boyfriends, marriage, even having the possibility of a family – normal life,' said Stuart, trailing away slightly.

Emily didn't look confused or frustrated at the response but instead turned her head to look out at the nearest street lamp. After a second or so she turned back, this time looking Stuart directly in the eye and speaking with a calm and caring voice. 'No one with a normal life could have done what you did. I couldn't have stripped down and rebuilt a car without help, let alone prepared it for a race. I couldn't have won a race like you did. The reason that trophy is in your house is because you won it. You and you alone did that. I read up on your condition, you know, after you told me about it. I find it incredible what you can do. Others could only but dream of being able to get inside minds like yours.'

Stuart froze for a second, thinking about what Emily had just said. 'You won't have me back, then,' said Stuart as Emily sighed.

'You were never with me in the first place, Stu. I always thought that I was helping you get into a relationship. I never realised that it was me you were trying to date,' said Emily.

Stuart went a little quiet and out of focus for a minute, staring straight ahead at the brick wall to the right of Emily's shoulder. 'Okay,' he said stiffly.

'Are you all right, Stu?' asked Emily.

'Yes, like I said. Normal life, I suppose,' said Stuart. Emily was now starting to get a little concerned.

'Try not to let it get to you, Stu. You're never going to be in a relationship if you try forcing yourself into it,' said Sophie, materialising to his left.

'Especially not with my brain,' said Stuart, turning to speak to Sophie.

Emily's eyes widened in surprise. 'Now I'm getting worried; you're talking to thin air now,' she said. Stuart realised too late that Emily couldn't see Sophie next to him.

'I have something I have to tell you,' said Stuart, as Emily seemed a little nervous. Emily nodded slightly as Stuart launched into his story of Sophie. He described how she was a part of his mind box mental software who helped him with relationships and understanding girls, emotions, and many other things besides.

When Stuart finally finished speaking, Emily's expression had changed from confusion to complete amazement. She hadn't spoken at all whilst Stuart had been talking but now had the voice to speak again.

'I never knew. So she lives inside you, this Sophie person?' said Emily, trying to get her head round the whole mental conundrum.

'She is me – well, a part of me, like when spiritual mediums have a spiritual guide. She's a guidance program,' replied Stuart, feeling a huge weight being lifted off his mind.

'Emily, there you are,' said a sudden voice. A youngish-looking man around Stuart's own age with jet-black hair and beard appeared at Emily's side.

'This is Derek. He's my boyfriend,' said Emily.

Stuart flinched at the sight of him but regained himself. 'You're busy. I'm so sorry to have bothered you. Have a pleasant day, Miss Green,' said Stuart, bowing a little. He turned and made his way back towards the main road, moving swiftly and silently.

'Who was that?' asked Derek, looking at Stuart as he walked away with his hands by his sides.

'That was Stuart. Excuse me,' said Emily suddenly. She slid out of the doorway after Stuart.

'Hey, Stu,' said Emily as Stuart turned to her. Before he could say a word, Emily hooked her arms around him and locked her lips onto his. For a brief moment she didn't let go as Stuart stood rooted to the spot. When she finally broke away, Stuart had bright red lips where Emily's lipstick had smudged.

'Oh, you got lipstick on you,' said Emily, blushing a little before taking a hankie out of her pocket and wiping it off of Stuart's face.

'No hard feelings, Stu. We can still be friends. I just thought you might have needed that to perk you up a bit,' said Emily. But before she could say another word, Stuart had locked both of his arms around her in a comforting hug. Emily's eyes watered a little. Stuart was hugging her so tightly she felt her eyes start bulging slightly, like a tree frog's would do. After what felt an age Stuart let go, allowing Emily to breath normally again.

'Thank you,' said Stuart slowly. Then without warning he turned and made off running at breakneck speed off down the road which led out of town towards the Robson farmhouse. Emily sighed before walking back towards the house, letting her blonde hair blow in the wind as she went.

Stuart sprinted all the way home until he finally came to a stop in the Robson farmyard. There was nobody else around. David was out with Rick across the other side of the county. Edward was running a steam train on the local miniature railway, and Abigail had been invited out to a friend's house for the day. The sun was high in the sky with not a cloud obscuring its view. It was at that point that the full reality of the situation that had unfolded just less than ten minutes earlier came to the front.

'She kissed me. She actually kissed me,' said Stuart, running his hand over his lips to feel where Emily had kissed him.

'I'm glad she understood,' said Sophie, putting one hand on his shoulder.

'I know – she's happy, and that's what matters,' said Stuart as Sophie smiled in agreement.

'So what now? Are you going to be riding on the Wheels of Thunder?' said Sophie.

Stuart walked over to the barn and slid the doors open, shining sunlight onto the UK flag covering Thunderbolt. But it was what was stood next to Thunderbolt that Stuart now had eyes for. Sophie's eyes widened in shock at the new vehicle that had joined the Land Rover, the Fordson tractor, and the Thunderbolt race car.

'I give you Black Bonnie,' said Stuart. The brand-new, 65- plate Triumph Bonneville T100 motorcycle gleamed, having been delivered less than two days earlier by Triumph motorcycles themselves, despite Abigail's pleading for Stuart not to own or even ride another motorcycle.

The cool new name 'Black Bonnie' imprinted on the side panels made the whole motorbike look amazing. Stuart ran his hand along the fuel tank and saddle, loving its every angle and feature. '865cc twin cylinder with twin fuel injectors disguised to look like carburettors,' said Stuart, rattling the information off like he was some sort of salesman for Triumph motorcycles.

'The open road is calling you,' said Sophie with a smile.

'I agree,' said Stuart. He grabbed his crash helmet and leather jacket off of the side bench and put them on before swinging himself onto Black Bonnie and flicking the starter switch on the handlebars. The engine purred into life with a low thumping sound like the Bonnevilles always did on tick-over.

The sound of the revving engine echoed around the barn as Stuart pulled the throttle slightly and went for the gear-changer. Black Bonnie rolled slowly forward into the bright barnyard. After closing and bolting both doors on the barn, he then remounted Black Bonnie, sliding his aviator sunglasses onto his face. Sophie grinned at his happiness.

'Coming for a ride?' asked Stuart. Sophie climbed up onto the rear pillion seat. The engine roared again as he selected first gear and rode off down the winding road, taking in the superb handling and effortless brilliance which only Triumph could deliver. With his newfound winning streak and effortless ability, maybe the world could see him for who he really was.

'Where we off to now?' said Sophie as Stuart came to a stop at the T-junction to the main road.

'Everywhere, Sophie my darling. Everywhere,' replied Stuart. He pulled away, heading off at speed up the winding road into the now-glaring midday sun. Black Bonnie effortlessly took every corner by storm, handling like a true British superbike. *Black Bonnie is go*, thought Stuart as the road opened up into a long, straight run. He felt the wind rushing past him out as he opened the throttle to full power. Black Bonnie accelerated faster than ever before, pushing past the point where even Sophie was tapping him on the shoulder and telling him to slow down. He closed the throttle all the way down, and Black Bonnie slowly cruised to a stop on the bridge overlooking the A10 north of Broxbourne.

Dismounting, Stuart wasn't surprised to see that Sophie had disappeared. *Due to fright*, Stuart thought as he sat overlooking the many cars and lorries speeding along underneath him. In fact, he sat there so long that it was almost dark before he moved away again heading for home, loving every second that Black Bonnie could deliver. Triumph was certainly the name not just of the make but of its rider as well. Stuart was a successful person who had taken on the impossible and won. To the select few who knew him, Stuart was the incredible and the mighty who fought with words of his own making. Impossible would never be an option.

The End

Epilogue

The True Story Behind the Real Wheels of Thunder

In the Words of the Author, Stuart Harvey

If you've been completely and utterly mind-boggled by reading this novel, then you have nothing to worry about. If you are someone who suffers from autism then reading and understanding this is what matters. If you're someone who doesn't, then please allow me to go into detail about the story behind *Wheels of Thunder*. I first come up with the idea when I was in my fourth year at secondary school, after a girl in my form group admitted to me that she was never truly in love with me and was already in a relationship with someone else. This came as a surprise to me, as my aim hadn't been a sexual relationship at all but just having someone to say hello to every day and to build on my confidence, which at the time wasn't brilliant.

This brought home the horrible truth that being on the autism spectrum wasn't going to be the walk in the park that I had once thought. It was then that the idea took off. This gave me the story line to start off with but not really anything else. The book was originally going to be called *Stinger* after the feeling of losing something very close to you. Bringing my love of cars into the mixture gave the story another line to go on, and so the title was changed to *Wheels of Thunder* instead. The first rough idea surfaced in late 2015 but was still missing a lot of the content due to the fact that the real-life events it was based on were ongoing.

The character known in this as Sophie is in a sense a part of the autistic system which can sometimes surface but at other times can remain dormant for the whole of your life. To some of us, having this mental guidance can be the difference between existence and extinction. Of course, the angels can often only be constructed in our minds, so if people turn around and say 'Your angel is like you,' there's more truth to that than people realise. Of course, I just use the term 'angel' just so it has a name. Others with the autism gene may call it by another name, but the same concept is still there through all of our minds. On the side of the motors, I do like cars. Well, 'like' is an understatement. I love them to bits.

The character Ben in the book is based on my real-life best friend, whom I met at secondary school. He was the one who got me into things like supercars, BBC's *Top Gear*, and the like. Before then my family were mainly train- and aircraft-orientated, having worked at an aircraft company in Hertfordshire for two generations. But for me it was my love of cars, bikes, and lorries that won through. In 2014 I started working for a bathroom company in Hertfordshire, which now in 2016 I still like a lot. I have taken a lot of inspiration from my new job into writing *Wheels of Thunder*. I hope to have a sequel to it or maybe even a prequel one day. As I always say, watch this space.

Thank you so much for reading. I hope that you have enjoyed the book and understood autism a little more through this depiction of a life with a learning difficulty.

CPSIA information can be obtained
at www.ICGtesting.com
Printed in the USA
LVHW040529200122
708837LV00002B/95